Inventorying Data to Support Army Harmful Behavior Prevention Metrics and Measures

KIRSTEN M. KELLER, KIMBERLY CURRY HALL, KELLY HYDE,
SIERRA SMUCKER, LINDA COTTRELL, GRACE TANG, HUNTER STOLL

Prepared for the United States Army
Approved for public release; distribution is unlimited.

For more information on this publication, visit **www.rand.org/t/RRA2368-1**.

About RAND

RAND is a research organization that develops solutions to public policy challenges to help make communities throughout the world safer and more secure, healthier and more prosperous. RAND is nonprofit, nonpartisan, and committed to the public interest. To learn more about RAND, visit www.rand.org.

Research Integrity

Our mission to help improve policy and decisionmaking through research and analysis is enabled through our core values of quality and objectivity and our unwavering commitment to the highest level of integrity and ethical behavior. To help ensure our research and analysis are rigorous, objective, and nonpartisan, we subject our research publications to a robust and exacting quality-assurance process; avoid both the appearance and reality of financial and other conflicts of interest through staff training, project screening, and a policy of mandatory disclosure; and pursue transparency in our research engagements through our commitment to the open publication of our research findings and recommendations, disclosure of the source of funding of published research, and policies to ensure intellectual independence. For more information, visit www.rand.org/about/research-integrity.

RAND's publications do not necessarily reflect the opinions of its research clients and sponsors.

Published by the RAND Corporation, Santa Monica, Calif.
© 2024 RAND Corporation
RAND® is a registered trademark.

Library of Congress Cataloging-in-Publication Data is available for this publication.
ISBN: 978-1-9774-1381-9

About This Report

This report documents research and analysis conducted as part of a project entitled *Inventorying Data to Support Harmful Behavior Prevention Metrics and Measures*, sponsored by the Deputy Chief of Staff, G-1, U.S. Army. The purpose of the project was to identify existing data being collected by the U.S. Army and by the U.S. Department of Defense (DoD) but accessible to the Army that can be used to measure progress toward the prevention of harmful behaviors.

This research was conducted within RAND Arroyo Center's Personnel, Training, and Health Program. RAND Arroyo Center, part of RAND, is a federally funded research and development center (FFRDC) sponsored by the United States Army.

RAND operates under a "Federal-Wide Assurance" (FWA00003425) and complies with the *Code of Federal Regulations for the Protection of Human Subjects Under United States Law* (45 CFR 46), also known as "the Common Rule," as well as with the implementation guidance set forth in DoD Instruction 3216.02. As applicable, this compliance includes reviews and approvals by RAND's Institutional Review Board (the Human Subjects Protection Committee) and by the U.S. Army. The views of sources utilized in this report are solely their own and do not represent the official policy or position of DoD or the U.S. government.

Acknowledgments

We begin by thanking our project sponsor, Dr. James Helis, and project action officer, Dr. Melinda Key-Roberts, of the Army Directorate of Prevention Resilience and Readiness (formerly the Army Resilience Directorate) for their continued guidance and support throughout the project. We are also particularly thankful for the support from and collaboration with Dr. Katherine Schaughency and Dr. Marjorie Dorak of the Integrated Prevention Division within the Army Directorate of Prevention Resilience and Readiness. We also thank the many subject-matter experts in DoD and the Army who participated in our interviews and helped us identify and understand relevant data sources on harmful behaviors.

Finally, we are very thankful to several RAND colleagues. First, we appreciate the continued support from the Arroyo Personnel, Training, and Health management team, Heather Krull and Katharina Best. We also thank Annie Brothers and Bella González, who provided research support on the project. In addition, Melissa Bauman provided valuable communications support to the project. We are also appreciative of the expert insights and reviews provided by Coreen Farris, Kimberly Hepner, Miriam Matthews, and Sarah Meadows. Finally, we are grateful for the technical reviews of this report provided by Stephanie Holliday, Rajeev Ramchand, and Maria Lytell. Their feedback helped to strengthen the content of the final product.

Summary

Having accurate data to better understand the occurrence and frequency of harmful behaviors, including their related risk and protective factors, is critical to the Army's primary prevention efforts of stopping harmful behaviors before they occur. This report focuses on data sources related to the harmful behaviors of domestic abuse, prohibited discrimination, sexual assault and sexual harassment, substance use,[1] and suicide.[2] The report documents information on 54 different data sources containing information related to these harmful behaviors. The report also identifies the following types of challenges with using these data sources that, if addressed, can help improve overall prevention efforts in the Army:

- **Data sources on the occurrence of harmful behaviors.** Data on harmful behaviors are often tracked in multiple different data sources and owned by different organizations, which limits the use of these data in obtaining a more comprehensive picture of harmful behaviors. Although confidential surveys can be used to estimate the true prevalence of harmful behaviors, these surveys can also have challenges (e.g., changing measures) and do not address all harmful behaviors (e.g., domestic abuse) at the time of this report.
- **Data collection on risk and protective factors.** Although numerous individual-level risk factors have been identified and are tracked in data sources, there are fewer factors tracked for higher levels, such as community-oriented (e.g., unit, installation, local community) or Army-level factors. Similarly, less is known and fewer data are collected regarding protective factors for many harmful behaviors.
- **Ability to analyze relevant data.** A lack of standardization can hinder analysis of trends over time and within demographic groups (e.g., race, ethnicity) and organizational units. In some cases, data sources might not even contain information needed to examine data at the organizational level. The ability to conduct longitudinal analyses can also be limited by changes in data collection procedures and the extent to which individuals can be tracked over time.
- **Data access issues.** There is a lack of common knowledge regarding which data sources are available, who has access to them, and how they are accessed. Concerns around data sensitivity and potential misinterpretation create a barrier to sharing data and the ability to have true integrated prevention.

---

[1] In addition to being a harmful behavior itself, substance use is also a risk factor for other harmful behaviors included in this study.

[2] The specific behaviors focused on in this report were based on sponsor guidance. The U.S. Department of Defense's *Prevention Plan of Action 2.0 2022–2024* (2022a) focuses on the harmful behaviors of sexual assault, harassment, retaliation, domestic abuse, suicide, and child abuse.

Contents

Tables

Inventorying Data to Support Army Harmful Behavior Prevention Metrics and Measures

In May 2022, the U.S. Department of Defense (DoD) released its *Prevention Plan of Action 2.0 2022–2024* (PPoA 2.0), which describes the department's strategic force-wide approach to "stopping incidents of self-directed harm and prohibited abuse and harm before they occur" (DoD, 2022a, p. 4). This approach focuses on primary prevention, which requires "understanding the current environment, determining the scope of the local problem, and assessing the organizational factors that enable prevention" (DoD, 2022a, p. 5). As the PPoA 2.0 notes, to do this effectively, DoD and the services will need access to data that can help identify the "prevalence (number of people impacted) and incidence (frequency of occurrence)" of harmful behaviors over time (DoD, 2022a, p. 6). The PPoA 2.0 also asserts the importance of identifying factors known to contribute to harmful behaviors or their prevention.

In addition, the PPoA 2.0 and *Army Integrated Prevention Advisory Group (I-PAG) Guide: Tactical* outline the need for integrated and accessible data systems to support prevention efforts (DoD, 2022a; U.S. Army Directorate of Prevention, Resilience and Readiness, 2022). "Measures of effectiveness and measures of performance for prevention planning and execution in the military environment are needed," and data must be "systematically captured, analyzed, interpreted, and shared, so that it provides timely and accurate information to inform decisions" (DoD, 2022a, p. 16). Of note, when considering data needs to support prevention efforts, the 2022 *Army Data Plan* outlines the Army's goal for data to be "visible, accessible, understandable, linked, trusted, interoperable and secure," which is represented by the acronym VAULTIS (Office of the Chief Information Officer, 2022, p. 5).

To better support and execute PPoA 2.0 and improve its own prevention efforts, the Army asked the RAND Arroyo Center to help identify existing data being collected by the Army and by DoD but accessible to the Army that can be used in support of the Army's harmful behavior prevention efforts at the headquarters level, as well as for commanders and prevention personnel. As part of this effort, the Army asked our RAND study team to explore and document key characteristics of relevant data sources related to harmful behaviors as well as identify gaps in or limitations to current data collection efforts.[3]

---

[3] The results from our effort have also been used to build an interactive data repository tool for Army users to help inform what metrics and measures can be supported by existing data and where new data need to be collected or better leveraged to support and evaluate the Army's efforts to prevent harmful behaviors. This tool will not be released to the public.

Study Scope and Approach

For the purposes of this study, we focus on the following harmful behaviors: domestic abuse, prohibited discrimination,[4] sexual assault and sexual harassment, substance use, and suicide.[5] DoD's definitions of each of these harmful behaviors can be found in Appendix A.

Because the goal of the study is to identify data that could be used to better support and evaluate the Army's efforts to prevent these harmful behaviors, we focus on identifying (1) data sources that document incidents or reports of harmful behaviors and (2) data that are designed to assess broader prevalence within the Army.[6]

In addition, we sought to identify data sources that contain information on risk factors and protective factors for each harmful behavior. *Risk factors* are defined by the Office of the Under Secretary of Defense for Personnel and Readiness as "[f]actors that increase the likelihood of self-directed harm and prohibited abusive or harmful acts," while *protective factors* are defined as "[i]ndividual or environmental characteristics, conditions, or behaviors that reduce the effects of stressful life events (e.g., inclusion, help-seeking behavior, financial literacy) . . . [which] increase the ability to avoid risks and promote healthy behaviors to thrive in all aspects of life" (Department of Defense Instruction [DoDI] 6400.09, 2020, pp. 30–31). In short, risk factors increase the likelihood that a person might experience or commit a harmful behavior, whereas protective factors lower that likelihood.

Risk and protective factors are sometimes simply the inverse of each other (e.g., being older lowers the risk of experiencing harmful behavior, while being younger increases it) but not always (e.g., being unmarried is a common risk factor for victimization of harmful behaviors, but being married is not always a protective factor). Moreover, for harmful behaviors that involve two individuals (a perpetrator and a victim), such as sexual assault and sexual harassment, risk and protective factors for *victimization* can be different from risk and protective factors for *perpetration*. For example, although gender is a risk factor for sexual assault victimization (e.g., being female) and perpetration (e.g., being male), the belief that rape is justified in certain circumstances is a risk factor only for sexual assault perpetration and unrelated to victimization (Chinman et al., 2021). Across the harmful behaviors we included in this study, researchers have identified several risk and protective factors that overlap at times. Some risk factors—being male, having a lower level of education, and having a mental health condition—are associated with all the harmful behaviors in this report. Others are specifically associated with one or two harmful behaviors (Wolters et al., 2023).

It was outside the scope of this study to conduct an in-depth review of all relevant risk and protective factors identified in research for the harmful behaviors we examined. In consultation with

---

[4] Prohibited discrimination is defined differently for the active-duty DoD and Army workforce than for the civilian DoD and Army workforce. These distinctions are explored in the Prohibited Discrimination section in this report.

[5] The decision to focus on these harmful behaviors was made in consultation with the study sponsor. We note that the PPoA 2.0 focuses on sexual assault, harassment, retaliation, domestic abuse, suicide, and child abuse.

[6] Because experiences of harmful behaviors are underreported, data only on reported incidents or cases fail to capture the true prevalence of a harmful behavior among the population of interest (DoD, 2019; Miller et al., 2023; Sadler et al., 2021). Therefore, DoD and the Army have taken steps to estimate prevalence through other sources, such as surveys that ask questions about specific behavioral experiences. Department of Defense Instruction (DoDI) 6400.09 defines prevalence as the "proportion of people in a population who have some attribute or condition at a given point in time or during a specified time period" (2022, p. 28).

our study sponsor, we leveraged recent research for the Army by Wolters et al. (2023), who used a multipronged approach to develop a map of crosscutting (i.e., shared or common) risk and protective factors in support of primary prevention for harmful behaviors across an Army-specific social-ecological model (SEM). The authors of that report focused on suicide, substance misuse, domestic violence, sexual harassment and assault, discrimination, and extremism, and they developed a definition for each behavior based on the DoD definition (when available) and civilian prevention literature.

Wolters and her co-authors developed an Army-specific SEM to organize their findings and situated risk and protective factors across several levels. The SEM levels are society (largest), Army, installation or community, unit, interpersonal, and individual. The authors reviewed the literature and substantiated 40 crosscutting risk factors and 15 crosscutting protective factors for the harmful behaviors; the majority of factors identified were at the individual level. Appendix B provides an overview of these crosscutting factors as well as key risk and protective factors specific to each harmful behavior examined in this report. Our analysis uses this framework for our assessment of risk and protective factors collected in the data sources. However, it is important to note that our review indicates whether a data source contains information identified as being a risk factor, protective factor, or both—but the validity and reliability of the particular measure of that risk or protective factor (including whether it is related to a particular harmful behavior) might still need to be assessed in many cases.[7]

Approach to Identifying Relevant Data Sources

To identify relevant data sources, we used a multipronged approach. Our primary data source was interviews conducted with subject-matter experts (SMEs) from DoD and the Army who oversee the programs responsible for the prevention of each of the harmful behaviors in our study. These programs and their representatives were initially identified through our sponsor, who made introductions and requested support for the study. To identify additional SMEs with knowledge of potentially relevant data sources, we then used a snowball sampling approach and asked our interviewees to suggest other SMEs with whom we should speak. In total, we spoke with 51 SMEs from across DoD and the Army from the offices listed in the box below.

---

[7] Wolters et al. (2023) also caution that it was beyond the scope of their work to conduct a rigorous meta-analysis identifying factors at six SEM levels for six behaviors. They recommend that the factors they identified as a framework for the Army should be modified as additional research on these factors is conducted.

DoD and Army Offices Included in Our Interviews

DoD:

- Defense Health Agency (DHA) Public Health
- Defense Suicide Prevention Office
- Office of People Analytics (OPA)
- Sexual Assault Prevention and Response Office
- Violence Prevention Cell

Army:

- Army Analytics Group (AAG)
- Army Research Institute
- Army Directorate of Prevention Resilience and Readiness,[a] which includes the Integrated Prevention Division (IPD)
- Center for Army Leadership (CAL)
- Equal Employment Opportunity (EEO)
- Equity and Inclusion Agency
- Manpower and Reserve Affairs (Quality of Life)
- Manpower and Reserve Affairs (Study to Assess Risk and Resilience in Service Members – Longitudinal Study [STARRS-LS])
- Medical Command (Family Advocacy Program)
- Military Equal Opportunity (MEO)
- Office of the Provost Marshal General
- Sexual Harassment/Assault Response and Prevention

[a] This was formerly the Army Resilience Directorate in G-1.

To supplement the information gathered from these interviews, we also reviewed relevant DoD and Army policy documents related to harmful behavior prevention and previously published studies conducted for DoD and the Army. The goal of these reviews was to identify potential additional data sources that might not have been raised during our interviews. We also interviewed five RAND experts who have studied harmful behaviors for DoD and the Army and have experience working with relevant data sources.

Finally, throughout this study, we worked closely with IPD representatives who were in the process of conducting their own review of potential data sources for use by the I-PAG, the Army's new integrated primary prevention workforce.[8] Although our review is intended to provide a deeper dive on key characteristics of a prioritized set of data sources considered most relevant to the prevention of harmful behaviors, the IPD has been putting together a broader list of all potential data sources within the Army. We conducted a crosswalk of our prioritized list of data sources with their much broader list and worked with our sponsor and the IPD representatives to ensure that our

---

[8] The IPD is a component of the G-9 Directorate of Prevention, Resilience, and Readiness. The I-PAG's objective is to "to build the service's integrated prevention system" that will "support leader-led efforts to improve policies, programs and practices intended to increase protective factors, build positive peer environments, and prevent harmful incidents and behaviors from occurring within the Army," as well as "implement integrated measures across the service that enable Soldiers, Civilians and their Family members to remain safe and focused on the mission at hand" (I-PAG, undated).

finalized list of data sources included those data sources considered most relevant to the prevention of harmful behaviors, based on the set of predetermined criteria outlined below.

Criteria for Inclusion and Exclusion

The Army and DoD have many different types of data sources with information about military members. Our intent with this study was not to capture all these data sources but to identify those that contain information directly related to the occurrence of the harmful behaviors that were the focus of this study and their risk and protective factors. In consultation with the sponsor, we developed the following inclusion criteria:

- **Data related to the occurrence of a harmful behavior and the risk and protective factors related to the harmful behaviors of our study.** In determining whether the data source includes information on risk or protective factors, we focused on those factors that were identified in a previous Army study (Wolters et al., 2023). We also included data sources that SMEs said they use to help assess risk and protective factors.
- **Owned by the Army or DoD.** Our goal was specifically to focus on data sources owned by the Army or owned by DoD but that the Army would be able to access. Therefore, we did not include data sources from public datasets (e.g., the Centers for Disease Control and Prevention), even if those might capture soldiers as part of their data collection.
- **Mentioned in a SME interview as a critical source of information.** To help scope the number of data sources included in our review, we focused on those data sources identified by SMEs as critically important to their work. As noted earlier, we also included data sources that were identified by IPD representatives as particularly relevant. There might be other data sources with relevant information, but our intent was to focus on the sources identified as most important for the harmful behaviors in our study.
- **Focus on active-duty personnel.** For our study, we did not gather information on data sources that were specific to civilians, reservists, or National Guard members.[9] As part of our review, we do note which components are included in the data sources we cover; in many cases, the sources include an assessment of the total force.[10]
- **Data recency.** Our goal was to focus on current data that would be most useful for Army efforts. Therefore, we did not include data sources that have been discontinued or that represent a single data collection event from years prior.

Finally, we note that although there are published reports that describe aggregate findings of estimated prevalence or risk and protective factors for many of these harmful behaviors, our focus is on the data sources underlying these reports. Therefore, our list does not include annual reports or peer-reviewed articles. We do, however, include relevant dashboards or platforms that provide users with an ability to access and manipulate data from the sources we identified (e.g., the Army's Commander's

---

[9] We include the civilian EEO iComplaints database as the civilian counterpart to the MEO database because active-duty military members might be identified as alleged perpetrators in the civilian EEO database.

[10] DoD and Army harmful behavior prevention plans focus on the total force. This effort is focused on active-duty members, but future efforts to identify data sources specific to civilians, reservists, and National Guard members would also be beneficial.

Risk Reduction Toolkit [CRRT] provides commanders with an interactive web-based tool that compiles data from multiple different data sources to help commanders assess data trends on a variety of risk factors).

Developing a Framework for Documenting Relevant Data Characteristics

To better understand existing data that can be used to measure progress toward the prevention of harmful behaviors, we developed a framework for documenting key characteristics of each data source. In identifying what key characteristics to include as part of our framework, we sought to document basic information on the type of harmful behavior and risk or protective factors assessed, as well as the extent to which the data could be leveraged to support prevention and measure progress. For example, based on sponsor input, we included the ability to aggregate or drill down by key demographics (e.g., gender, race, ethnicity), pay grade, and organizational level. We also included the extent to which the data source was accessible to different stakeholder groups and could be linked to other data sources. Finally, we also included key strengths and limitations of each data source (e.g., ability to estimate prevalence, quality of data). An overview of our full documentation framework is contained in Appendix C.

Overview of Key Harmful Behavior Data Sources

We identified and documented a total of 54 data sources that contain information on domestic abuse, prohibited discrimination, sexual assault and sexual harassment, substance use, or suicide in the Army, as well as several Army personnel databases that, although not focused on harmful behaviors, include relevant demographic or other background information that represent important risk and protective factors.[11] The full list of these data sources with a high-level summary of each is available in Appendix D.

As noted previously, these data sources reflect what SMEs consider the most-critical data sources for these harmful behaviors.[12] Many of these data sources contain information on more than one harmful behavior. Table 1 displays the number of data sources with information on the occurrence of each harmful behavior in scope and the number of data sources that contain information on the risk and protective factors associated with each harmful behavior.

---

[11] To help the Army house and effectively use the information in our framework, we created an interactive data repository tool. This tool does not contain data on harmful behaviors but allows Army users to explore available data sources relevant to prevention of harmful behaviors, including their risk and protective factors. Users can filter available data sources by various characteristics, including but not limited to the type of harmful behavior (e.g., sexual assault, suicide), whether the data source includes information about risk or protective factors, and type of data source (e.g., survey, platform), and then users can view detailed information about each relevant data source. Furthermore, because data sources evolve, the tool is designed to allow Army SMEs with the necessary permissions to update the tool as needed when new data sources become available or when the types of information collected in a data source change. The tool will be of interest to many different types of Army users, including personnel involved in prevention efforts, researchers, and commanders. The tool is intended to help Army users easily identify available relevant data sources, including data at the individual level and dashboards that aggregate data across various sources, that can support efforts related to the prevention of harmful behaviors.

[12] We note that five data sources were added to our list based on discussions with IPD representatives.

Table 1. Number of Data Sources with Information on Each Harmful Behavior

Type of Information	Domestic Abuse	Prohibited Discrimination	Sexual Assault	Sexual Harassment	Substance Use	Suicide
Any information	37	26	42	46	41	43
Occurrence of harmful behavior	19	14	24	20	33	24
Risk factors	36	24	41	43	40	40
Protective factors	13	19	20	20	23	23

Overview of Key Characteristics Across Harmful Behavior Data Sources

In the following sections, we provide an overview of our categories of data sources, including the extent to which the data sources vary regarding the key characteristics documented in our framework. We then provide more-specific details regarding data sources relevant to each harmful behavior, noting key limitations or gaps in the available data. We note that data sources documented within this report represent a snapshot at the time of this study. Based on our SME discussions, DoD and the Army are continually refining their data collection efforts to better meet prevention needs.

Data Types

We identified four unique categories of data sources: *surveys*, *assessments*, *records*, and *platforms*.

- Surveys contain self-reported information derived from individual responses (e.g., the Workplace and Gender Relations Survey of Military Members: Active Component).
- Assessments contain evaluations of an individual by others, such as peers or subordinates (e.g., the Command Assessment Program Peer and Subordinate Assessments sponsored by the CAL).
- Records contain information regarding an individual's interactions with a provider for medical services or agencies, such as law enforcement (e.g., the Army Law Enforcement Reporting and Tracking System [ALERTS], which tracks records of interactions with law enforcement agencies), or officially reported incidents that are referred to health, law enforcement, or other agencies (e.g., Defense Casualty Information Processing System, [DCIPS]).[13]

---

[13] In other words, we classify data sources as records if they contain official documentation of an individual's interaction(s) with any organization or administrative process. Many of the data sources described in our repository exist to record the proceedings of a particular program or administrative process and contain information on harmful behaviors, risk factors, and protective factors that relate to the purpose of that program or process. The definition of *records* is broad because many types of programs and processes overlap with harmful behaviors and their risk and protective factors (e.g., health service providers, law enforcement agencies, prevention programs targeting a particular harmful behavior). The common thread among all data sources we classify as records is that they contain official records of some type of proceeding (e.g., a medical appointment, an arrest, a harassment complaint, an emergency room visit, completion of a substance misuse prevention program curriculum), whereas survey and assessment data sources contain information proactively collected on a subject from a group of individuals independently of any particular event. This has important implications for the ability to estimate prevalence (as opposed to reported incidence) of a

- Platforms provide an interface to visualize and access data from several different sources within the same environment (e.g., the CRRT, which provides a user-friendly visualization of several source datasets related to harmful behavior incidents and risks, and Advana, which "pulls data from hundreds of business systems to make it discoverable, understandable, and usable for advanced analytics" [Defense Logistics Agency Information Operations, 2022]).[14]

Using these categorizations, we identified a total of 12 survey data sources, nine assessment data sources, 16 record data sources, and 17 platform data sources. The following box provides an overview of the specific data sources within each category.

Data Sources, by Type

Survey data sources:

- Active-Duty Spouse Survey
- Behavioral Health Pulse (BH Pulse)
- CAL's Annual Study of Army Leadership (CASAL)
- Defense Organizational Climate Survey (DEOCS)
- Health Related Behaviors Survey (HRBS)
- QuickCompass of Sexual Assault Responders (QSAR)
- Service Academy Gender Relations (SAGR) survey
- Status of Forces Survey (SOFS)
- Study to Assess Risk and Resilience in Service Members – Longitudinal Study (STARRS-LS)
- Unit Risk Inventory (URI) and Re-integration Unit Risk Inventory (R-URI) surveys
- Workplace and Equal Opportunity (WEO) survey
- Workplace and Gender Relations Survey of Military Members: Active Component (WGRA)

Assessment data sources:

- Army Readiness Assessment Program (ARAP)
- Azimuth Check
- Behavioral and Social Health Self-Assessment Tool (BSH SAT)
- Career-Long Assessments: Athena

---

harmful behavior from these data sources, which is further discussed in the "Overview of Data Sources for Each Harmful Behavior" section of this report.

[14] Data catalogs, such as Advana, provide a unified environment to search for authoritative data sources, while data visualization platforms, such as the CRRT and Joint Analytical Real-Time Virtual Information Sharing System (JARVISS), eliminate the need to obtain access to, clean, and combine disparate data sources. From a harmful behavior measurement and prevention perspective, this means easier access to more complete information within a harmful behavior (e.g., ability to see recorded past incidents and risk factors for future incidents of sexual assault in the same place) and across harmful behaviors (e.g., using the CRRT to see substance use behaviors from the Drug and Alcohol Management Information System [DAMIS] and suicidal ideation records from the Department of Defense Suicide Event Report [DoDSER] or Military Health System Management Analysis and Reporting Tool [M2] side-by-side). Importantly, because platforms are built on top of existing data, these advantages are achieved with minimal or no changes to the collection or recording procedures of the underlying data sources. Although both data catalogs and data visualization platforms provide access to other datasets, the design of each might be more suitable for different use cases. Data catalogs might require raw data files for highly specific or complex analyses and are designed for researchers and other users who are comfortable using raw data, while data visualization platforms are designed more for lay users such as commanders who might not have the time or technical experience to analyze raw data.

- Command Assessment Program Peer and Subordinate Assessments (Lieutenant Colonel Army Commander Evaluation Tool, Colonel Army Commander Evaluation Tool, Army Leader Assessment Tool, Enlisted Leader Assessment Tool)
- Community Strengths and Themes Assessment (CSTA)
- Medical Readiness Assessment Tool (MRAT)
- Periodic Health Assessment (PHA)
- Post-Deployment Health Assessment (PDHA) and Post-Deployment Health Re-Assessment (PDHRA)

Record data sources:

- Army Crime Report
- Armed Forces Medical Examiner System (AFMES)
- Army Law Enforcement Reporting and Tracking System (ALERTS)
- Behavioral Health Data Portal (BHDP)
- Defense Casualty Information Processing System (DCIPS)
- DHA Medical Operational Data System (MODS) Electronic Profiling System (e-Profile)
- Defense Sexual Assault Incident Database (DSAID)
- Department of Defense Suicide Event Report (DoDSER)
- Drug and Alcohol Management Information System (DAMIS)
- Equal Employment Opportunity (EEO) iComplaints
- Family Advocacy Program (FAP) Central Registry
- Family Advocacy System of Records (FASOR)
- Integrated Case Reporting System (ICRS)
- Military and Family Life Counseling (MFLC) data
- Military Equal Opportunity (MEO) database
- Military Justice Online (MJO)

Platform data sources:

- Advana
- Army Safety Management Information System (ASMIS 2.0)
- Behavioral and Social Health Outcomes Practice Request for Information (BSHOP RFI) Database
- Commander's Risk Reduction Toolkit (CRRT)
- Defense Medical Epidemiology Database (DMED)
- Defense Medical Surveillance System (DMSS)
- DEOCS Commanders Dashboard
- Joint Analytical Real-Time Virtual Information Sharing System (JARVISS)
- Law Enforcement Defense Data Exchange (LE D-DEx)
- Military Health System Data Repository (MDR)
- Military Health System Management Analysis and Reporting Tool (MHS MART or M2)
- On-Site Installation Evaluation (OSIE) DEOCS
- OSIE Resilience Index
- Person-Event Data Environment (PDE)
- Strategic Management System (SMS) Army Suicide Prevention Program (ASPP)
- SMS drug testing
- SMS Sexual Harassment/Assault Response and Prevention (SHARP)

Frequency of Data Collection

The frequency of data collection varies largely by the type of data source. For example, the frequency of survey data collection depends on how often the survey is administered, and most surveys take place annually or every two to three years. Most assessment data sources are updated on a rolling basis when the assessments occur, but aggregated assessment results might be produced annually. Similarly, most record-type data sources are updated in real time, but access to the underlying real-time data is often restricted to specific individuals or institutions, and more broadly available derivative data products (e.g., aggregated reports) are produced monthly or annually. Finally, the frequency of a platform data source's collection depends on the frequencies of its underlying datasets; in most cases, the underlying data are queried directly by the platform, so the platform itself does not limit the update frequency.

Units of Observation

As would be expected, each observation in the underlying data sources varies by type and purpose. For all surveys, each observation in the underlying full-access data is an individual survey respondent. In assessment data, each observation is an evaluation of an individual by another individual or group of individuals. In record data, each observation is an interaction with a particular service or agency, which might be voluntary (e.g., a doctor appointment for illness treatment) or involuntary (e.g., a law enforcement case resulting from a report of sexual assault). Finally, in platform data, each observation depends on the structure of the platform. For large data repositories, such as the PDE that integrates data on Army and DoD personnel from more than 50 sources, each observation (usually individual level) depends on the dataset within the repository, while for data visualization dashboards, such as the CRRT, it can be an individual, a unit, or another level of aggregation, depending on the view selected.

Demographics and Organizational Identifiers

Based on sponsor input, as a key part of our framework, we also examined the extent to which each data source contained information that would allow the data to be analyzed based on demographic characteristics (i.e., race, ethnicity, gender) and could be aggregated to different organizational levels (e.g., unit vs. command). Understanding demographic differences related to harmful behaviors, as well as being able to identify potential differences by organizational level and location, are critical to prevention efforts. To conduct analyses with a data source in which the unit of analysis is an aggregation of the units of observation, such as calculating the difference in sexual assault reports by installation or command, the data must identify the group to which each observation belongs. In the case of fully anonymous survey data where no identifying information of any kind is collected, this analysis is not possible. For all other sources of data, the feasibility of conducting aggregated analyses depends on the analyst's access to these group identifiers. For some survey, assessment, or record data sources, demographic group identifiers, such as age, gender, marital status, or race and ethnicity, are already built into the dataset and can be easily aggregated. However, racial and ethnic categories might not be standardized across all data sources, limiting the ability to make such comparisons across data sources.

Organizational data, such as unit identification and installation, are less commonly collected and not always standardized across years and data sources, which makes analyses at this level more difficult. In these cases, the data may be linkable to personnel data, such as the Integrated Total Army Personnel Database (iTAPDB), if the user is able to obtain a unique identifier that allows the datasets to be merged, but this process requires significant effort and technical skills to link accurately. Furthermore, several SMEs told us that even if we could link by individuals, we still may not be able to analyze data by location if we cannot identify where the individual was located at the time of data collection (e.g., if a soldier received treatment at a military treatment facility not associated with their duty station). Thus, because data are often collected for specific purposes beyond prevention (e.g., medical records), the data might not lend itself to analysis by demographics and location, in particular. In some cases, a linked version of a dataset might be available via a platform that is designed with particular end users in mind. For example, individuals with access to the CRRT can use it to obtain prelinked information from the 19+ data sources it integrates without having to obtain and merge those data sources themselves.

Potential for Analyses over Time

All the data sources we identified contain multiple years of data and are either actively being updated or have planned updates. As a result, analyses over time at an aggregated level, such as calculating year-over-year trends in overall occurrences of harmful behaviors in the Army, are feasible using any of the data sources we identified. Some survey data sources, such as the HRBS, offer weights that can be used to derive estimates representative of the broader Army or DoD population, including those who did not respond to the survey; these weights can be used to make more-robust comparisons across years in which the sample or response rate might have differed. In surveys without weights, comparisons across time might be confounded by changes in the sampling frame or response rates over time. For example, if female soldiers are more likely to be victims of sexual assault, occurrences of sexual assault might appear to decrease in a year of survey data if the response rate among women is lower in that year.

Additionally, surveys can be limited in making aggregated comparisons over time depending on the consistency of the constructs being measured and the underlying items used to measure those constructs. For example, in 2020, the DEOCS underwent a significant redesign, making comparisons over time difficult. Prior to the redesign, DEOCS 4.1 included questions on hazing and bullying, but these questions were eliminated in the redesigned DEOCS 5.0. Conversely, questions on workplace hostility were added to DEOCS 5.0 that were not captured on the DEOCS 4.1. Similarly, the 2018 WGRA included questions on bystander intervention, unit culture, and unit climate, whereas the 2016 WGRA did not.

Furthermore, analyses over time of individuals or groups, such as identifying repeated harmful behaviors by an individual, are possible only if the user is able to uniquely identify individuals across years of the data. Although unique individual identifiers are often present in data sources, access to these identifiers is usually restricted to limit disclosure of personal identifiable information and protected health information. For example, the CRRT, which displays information from several datasets relating to harmful behaviors and risk factors linked to the individual's identity, is exclusively available to commanders and shows information only on individuals within each commander's purview. For analyses that would not require the actual identity of each individual, deidentified data that replace actual identifiers (e.g., names, Social Security numbers) with unique keys (e.g., arbitrary strings of text or numbers) might be available, such as the deidentified STARRS-LS survey data available from the Inter-university Consortium for Political and Social Research (ICPSR).

Another limitation to consider when trying to perform analyses of individuals or groups over time is that, particularly for data sources that are records, the data might not contain every occurrence of a harmful behavior affecting a particular individual. For example, underreporting is relevant when trying to identify repeat victims or perpetrators of harmful behaviors. Not all occurrences of harmful behaviors are reported, and data sources associated with particular agencies (e.g., case management databases) or regulatory requirements might be affected by changes in assessment or reporting requirements over time.[15] Repeated surveys, which are confidential (and for which participants have high confidence in the confidentiality), might be more likely to capture the full history of harmful behavior incidents involving an individual; however, many of the surveys in our repository are updated every one to three years, meaning that repeat incidents within a year may not be separable (i.e., a person answers "Yes" to a question about a harmful behavior, but it is not clear how many times it occurred or exactly when). Additionally, when an individual does not complete the survey in a given year, a large gap in the known history of that individual occurs, assuming the survey collects information that is able to track individuals over time. A complementary "pulse survey" approach, which asks the same brief set of questions about harmful behaviors repeatedly in regular intervals, might balance the reporting likelihood advantages of surveys and the higher update frequency of records.

Data Access

The permissions required to access data also vary by type of data, and many data sources feature tiers of access for different individuals, depending on their credentials and intended use for the data. These tiers of access often involve different levels of granularity. For example, aggregated results of the WGRA are publicly available, while de-identified microdata containing individual responses are available only with permission from the OPA and only for certain approved purposes.

In all cases, access to individually identifiable data is narrowly restricted to a small group of approved individuals; the specific group with access depends on the particular data source. For example, on the one hand, the CRRT is designed specifically for commanders. On the other hand, datasets designed for research purposes that contain individually identifiable information allow access only to scientists within the sponsoring agency of the data source (as in the CAL's assessments) or to researchers who have received direct permission from the sponsoring agency.

Challenges regarding data access were frequently raised during our discussions with SMEs. We were told that, given the sensitive nature of certain types of data and their related privacy and identifiability concerns, many offices are very cautious about sharing data and are often willing to release data only at an aggregate level, if at all. These data sensitivities are obviously very important. However, we were told that this extreme caution also presents a barrier to the Army's more integrated

---

[15] In other cases, there might be multiple records (e.g., suicide ideation, suicide attempt) from the same soldier that will need to be linked together so that soldiers are not double counted.

approach to prevention because such prevention efforts end up being siloed and potentially valuable sources of data are not shared. Both the PPoA 2.0 (DoD, 2022a) and the *Army I-PAG Guide: Tactical* describe an integrated primary prevention approach, which promotes prevention activities that "simultaneously address multiple harmful behaviors or the inclusion of prevention activities across harmful behaviors into a cohesive, comprehensive approach that promotes unity of effort, avoids unnecessary duplication, and lessens training fatigue" (U.S. Army Directorate of Prevention, Resilience and Readiness, 2022, p. 5). In other words, this integrated approach recognizes that many harmful behaviors have shared risk and protective factors and emphasizes the importance of targeting those shared factors.

Additionally, the SMEs were concerned that a lack of knowledge about which data are available and access issues to key data sources can result in people using whatever data sources they do have readily accessible, which might not be the best sources of information for the intended purposes (e.g., using incident databases that rely on victims having made formal reports of experiencing a harmful behavior instead of using data from anonymous or confidential surveys that can provide more-accurate and reliable prevalence estimates). In our own efforts to identify data sources, it was difficult to find publicly available information on who was allowed access to a data source and how to gain access (e.g., whom to contact to request access permission).

Overview of Data Sources for Each Harmful Behavior

In the following sections, we summarize our findings specific to each type of harmful behavior within the scope of our study. For each type of harmful behavior, we identify key data sources, the extent to which data sources are available that measure related risk and protective factors, and any gaps in measurement. Based on our SME discussions and internal team analyses, we also note key strengths and limitations of these data sources.

Domestic Abuse

Data sources containing information on the occurrence of domestic abuse, related risk factors, and related protective factors are listed in Table 2.

Table 2. Data Sources for Domestic Abuse, by Type

Data Source	Occurrence	Risk Factors	Protective Factors
Survey Data Sources			
Active-Duty Spouse Survey		x	
Behavioral Health Pulse (BH Pulse)	x	x	x
Defense Organizational Climate Survey (DEOCS)		x	
Health Related Behaviors Survey (HRBS)		x	
Service Academy Gender Relations (SAGR) survey		x	x

Data Source	Occurrence	Risk Factors	Protective Factors
Study to Assess Risk and Resilience in Service Members – Longitudinal Study (STARRS-LS)	x	x	x
Unit Risk Inventory (URI) and Re-integration Unit Risk Inventory (R-URI) Surveys	x	x	
Assessment Data Sources			
Azimuth Check		x	x
Behavioral and Social Health Self-Assessment Tool (BSH SAT)		x	x
Community Strengths and Themes Assessment (CSTA)		x	x
Periodic Health Assessment (PHA)		x	x
Post-Deployment Health Assessment (PDHA) and Post-Deployment Health Re-Assessment (PDHRA)		x	
Record Data Sources			
Armed Forces Medical Examiner System (AFMES)		x	
Army Crime Report	x	x	
Army Law Enforcement Reporting and Tracking System (ALERTS)	x	x	
Behavioral Health Data Portal (BHDP)	x	x	
Defense Health Agency (DHA) Medical Operational Data System (MODS) Electronic Profiling System (e-Profile)		x	
Drug and Alcohol Management Information System (DAMIS)		x	
Family Advocacy Program (FAP) Central Registry	x		
Family Advocacy System of Records (FASOR)	x	x	
Military and Family Life Counseling (MFLC) data	x	x	
Military Justice Online (MJO)	x	x	
Platform Data Sources			
Advana	x	x	x
Army Safety Management Information System (ASMIS 2.0)		x	
Behavioral and Social Health Outcomes Practice Request for Information (BSHOP RFI) Database		x	
Commander's Risk Reduction Toolkit (CRRT)	x	x	
Defense Medical Epidemiology Database (DMED)	x	x	

Data Source	Occurrence	Risk Factors	Protective Factors
Defense Medical Surveillance System (DMSS)		x	
DEOCS Commanders Dashboard		x	
Joint Analytical Real-Time Virtual Information Sharing System (JARVISS)	x	x	
Law Enforcement Defense Data Exchange (LE D-DEx)	x	x	
Military Health System Data Repository (MDR)	x	x	x
Military Health System Management Analysis and Reporting Tool (MHS MART or M2)	x	x	x
Office of the Secretary of Defense (OSD) On-Site Installation Evaluation (OSIE) DEOCS		x	x
OSIE Resilience Index	x	x	x
Person-Event Data Environment (PDE)	x	x	x
Strategic Management System (SMS) drug testing		x	

Our SMEs indicated that the primary source of information on domestic abuse in the Army is data collected by the FAP. Several data sources, including DoD's FAP Central Registry, contain information on FAP cases and investigations that gets summarized in annual reports. Within the Army, domestic abuse information can be found in the FASOR. Information on domestic abuse cases not yet documented by FAP or FASOR might also be available through law enforcement agency data (e.g., ALERTS, JARVISS), medical services data (e.g., MHS MART or M2, MDR), and behavioral health assessments and consultations (e.g., BH Pulse, BSH SAT). Additionally, the URI anonymously asks Army personnel whether they physically assaulted their partner in the last year. BH Pulse, BSH SAT, and URI provide data at the unit level. However, because these data collections are only done by request or administered at different times (e.g., the URI is administered to units at different times based on their deployment schedule), data from these sources are not intended to be used to estimate Army-wide prevalence of domestic abuse at any given time.

At the time of this report, there were no comprehensive studies of domestic abuse prevalence in the Army or DoD (Miller et al., 2023), and the PPoA 2.0 notes DoD's lack of methods to fully assess the prevalence of domestic abuse (DoD, 2022a, p. 6). Notably, a 2021 U.S. Government Accountability Office (GAO) report found that one data record of alleged domestic abuse for the Army can represent multiple allegations, which sometimes results in an undercount of the number of allegations received. Additionally, the 2021 GAO report found that installation FAP personnel who were responsible for screening initial allegations of domestic abuse had been, in some cases, inappropriately screening out incidents that did meet DoD's definition of domestic abuse, which potentially contributed to an undercount of incidents. Furthermore, the 2021 GAO report found that the Army had no service-level monitoring of these installation-level screening decisions. In short, being able to provide accurate prevalence estimates of domestic abuse within the Army is a critical gap.

The risk factors for domestic abuse that are tracked in the data sources we identified include demographic information (e.g., gender, age, pay grade), family history of domestic abuse incidents, deployment history, mental well-being, and financial stress (Wolters et al., 2023). These risk factors can be found in personnel databases and self-reported surveys of Army personnel, such as the HRBS and SAGR survey, or their spouses through the Active-Duty Spouse Survey. Information on history of domestic abuse incidents might also be available from law enforcement or health data if these past incidents resulted in interactions with law enforcement agencies or medical services.

Although information on the risk factors of domestic abuse is available, information on protective factors is somewhat lacking. Notably, the framework of risk and protective factors from previous research (see Wolters et al., 2023) that is the basis of our analysis identifies protective factors that are difficult to quantify outside tailored survey measures. Protective factors tracked in the data sources we identified include family, social, and community connectedness, cohesion, and support. More individual-level information on life skills identified as protective factors from domestic abuse perpetration, including empathy, decisionmaking, and problem-solving capabilities, might benefit future analyses of domestic abuse risk in the Army. Additionally, more comprehensive surveys of the spouses of Army personnel and exploration of other methods to collect data from them might help to identify emerging domestic abuse risks and incidents more quickly. Recent research recommends strategies for measuring and evaluating domestic abuse prevention efforts (see Miller et al., 2023). For example, additional data collection efforts to support the prevention of domestic abuse could include implementing confidential population surveys of service members and their spouses or partners to measure such items as understanding of domestic abuse and its risk factors; experiences with domestic abuse; awareness of and attitudes toward domestic abuse prevention activities, resources, and reporting channels; barriers to help-seeking; and command buy-in or involvement in prevention (Miller et al., 2023).[16]

Prohibited Discrimination

Data sources containing information on the occurrence of prohibited discrimination, related risk factors, and related protective factors are listed in Table 3.

Table 3. Data Sources for Prohibited Discrimination, by Type

Data Source	Occurrence	Risk Factors	Protective Factors
Survey Data Sources			
BH Pulse	x	x	x
CASAL		x	x
DEOCS		x	x
HRBS		x	
STARRS-LS	x	x	x
URI and R-URI	x	x	x

---

[16] Being able to include spouses or dependents in surveys can extend approval times because they are members of the public. Our SMEs indicated that this delay has resulted in this subpopulation being excluded from previous studies.

Data Source	Occurrence	Risk Factors	Protective Factors
WEO survey	x	x	x
WGRA	x	x	x
Assessment Data Sources			
ARAP		x	x
BSH SAT		x	x
Career-Long Assessments: Athena		x	x
Command Assessment Program Peer and Subordinate Assessments (Lieutenant Colonel Army Commander Evaluation Tool, Colonel Army Commander Evaluation Tool, Army Leader Assessment Tool, Enlisted Leader Assessment Tool)		x	x
CSTA		x	x
PHA		x	x
Record Data Sources			
ALERTS	x		
BHDP	x	x	
DHA MODS e-Profile		x	
EEO iComplaints	x		
MEO database	x	x	
MJO	x	x	
Platform Data Sources			
Advana	x	x	x
CRRT	x	x	x
DEOCS Commanders Dashboard		x	x
OSIE DEOCS		x	x
OSIE Resilience Index	x	x	x
PDE	x	x	x

For data on prohibited discrimination (i.e., disparate treatment of an individual or group on the basis of race, color, national origin, religion, sex, gender identity, or sexual orientation),[17] our SMEs identified that the primary sources of information on reported incidents of prohibited discrimination

---

[17] We do not include a specific focus on bullying or hazing as part of this review, although targets of bullying and hazing can be based on protected categories for discrimination.

in the Army are those managed by the Army's Equity and Inclusion Agency. These data sources include the MEO database, which tracks prohibited discrimination complaints for military members, and the EEO iComplaints database, which tracks prohibited discrimination complaints initiated by civilians.[18] (These databases also separately track and collect reports of harassment; for the MEO database, this includes all types of harassment related to protected categories except for sexual harassment, and for EEO iComplaints, this includes all types of harassment complaints, including sexual harassment.) EEO prohibited discrimination complaints are reported annually to the Equal Employment Opportunity Commission.

As of the writing of this report (May 2024), planning was underway to integrate the MEO database into the ICRS. According to our SMEs, the goal of this change is to standardize data collection and tracking, improve reporting accuracy, and unify prohibited discrimination and harassment tracking under one system for military members. The new system will also enable access to more up-to-date data, whereas the current system provides only quarterly snapshots. While waiting for integration into ICRS, MEO prohibited discrimination complaints were being tracked in detailed spreadsheets by the Army's Equity and Inclusion Agency, functioning as the MEO database, at the time when this report was written. Our SMEs also reported that there is no DoD-wide MEO system to integrate prohibited discrimination complaints across all the military services.

Several DoD-level surveys also provide information about prohibited discrimination. Among them, the WGRA assesses gender discrimination, and the WEO survey assesses rates of racial or ethnic discrimination and harassment. The 2017 WEO survey also included two items on religious discrimination and two items on sexual orientation discrimination (DoD, OPA, undated-a). The SAGR survey is also designed to provide official prevalence estimates for gender discrimination among students at the academies. These surveys are administered at the DoD level and include the Army alongside the other service branches. In addition to these DoD-level surveys, the DEOCS, which provides unit-level data, assesses racially harassing behaviors and sexist behaviors as part of the nine risk factors it measures. The Army's URI also includes a single item on discrimination, asking the extent to which the respondent has been discriminated against by someone in their unit because of their race, religion, national origin, gender, or perceived sexual orientation.

As mentioned earlier, our SMEs noted that although these surveys are conducted on a regular basis, the survey items can change, which limits longitudinal assessments. In addition, some of these data sources have significant limitations. For example, the WEO survey has a very small sample size, and even though this survey is weighted, the weight might not be stable and could yield imprecise estimates. The DEOCS has other limitations, as described earlier. Furthermore, although the 2017 WEO survey contains two items each on discrimination due to religion and sexual orientation, these protected categories are not assessed to the same degree as racial or ethnic and gender discrimination.

Tracked risk and protective factors of prohibited discrimination include such demographics as gender, race, ethnicity, educational attainment, and sexual orientation. The DEOCS measures relevant unit-level factors, such as inclusion and leadership. The WEO survey also includes relevant

---

[18] MEO policy defines prohibited discrimination as on the basis of "race, color, national origin, religion, sex (including pregnancy), gender identity, or sexual orientation" (DoDI 1350.02, 2022, p. 38). EEO policy defines prohibited discrimination in employment as on the basis of "race, color, religion, sex, national origin, reprisal, disability, age, sexual orientation, gender identity, status as a parent, or other impermissible basis" (Army Regulation 690-12, 2019, p. 3).

measures of risk and protective factors, such as diversity and inclusion climate and items on attitudes or beliefs about race and ethnicity (e.g., the 2017 WEO survey included "Do you agree with the ideals of organizations that . . . point out the dangers of racial/ethnic diversity?" [DoD, OPA, undated-a]). As we discuss more in the next section on sexual assault and harassment, the 2021 WGRA was also designed to measure risk factors for gender discrimination (DoD, OPA, undated-c). Regarding organizational climate survey measures, one SME noted that although climate is intended to measure *shared* perceptions, individuals report their *individual* perceptions, meaning that there is no assessment as to whether these perceptions are shared across members within the unit or command.

Finally, much of the data source information on prohibited discrimination in the Army pertains to either victimization or perceptions of how prohibited discrimination is addressed or prevented. Other than the few items in the WEO survey, we did not identify a major data source focused on beliefs or attitudes about gender, race and ethnicity, or other demographic characteristics that might lead to discriminatory behavior. Additional information on belief- or attitude-based risk factors for the perpetration of prohibited discrimination might help anticipate future occurrences of prohibited discrimination.

Sexual Assault and Sexual Harassment

Data sources containing information on the occurrence of sexual assault and sexual harassment, their related risk factors, and their related protective factors are listed in Tables 4 and 5.

Table 4. Data Sources for Sexual Assault, by Type

Data Source	Occurrence	Risk Factors	Protective Factors
Survey Data Sources			
BH Pulse	x	x	x
CASAL		x	x
DEOCS	x	x	x
HRBS		x	
QSAR		x	
SAGR survey	x	x	x
STARRS-LS	x	x	x
URI and R-URI	x	x	x
WGRA	x	x	x
Assessment Data Sources			
ARAP		x	x
BSH SAT		x	x
Career-Long Assessments: Athena		x	x

Data Source	Occurrence	Risk Factors	Protective Factors
Command Assessment Program Peer and Subordinate Assessments		X	X
CSTA		X	X
PHA		X	X
PDHA and PDHRA		X	
Record Data Sources			
AFMES		X	
Army Crime Report	X	X	
ALERTS	X	X	
BHDP	X	X	
DAMIS		X	
DHA MODS e-Profile		X	
DSAID	X	X	
FASOR		X	
MFLC Data	X	X	
MJO	X	X	
Platform Data Sources			
Advana	X	X	X
ASMIS 2.0		X	
BSHOP RFI Database	X	X	
CRRT	X		
DEOCS Commanders Dashboard	X	X	X
DMED	X	X	
DMSS		X	
JARVISS	X	X	
LE D-DEx	X	X	
MDR	X	X	X
M2	X	X	X
OSIE DEOCS		X	X
OSIE Resilience Index	X	X	X
PDE	X	X	X

Data Source	Occurrence	Risk Factors	Protective Factors
SMS drug testing		x	
SMS SHARP	x	x	

Table 5. Data Sources for Sexual Harassment, by Type

Data Source	Occurrence	Risk Factors	Protective Factors
Survey Data Sources			
BH Pulse	x	x	x
CASAL		x	x
DEOCS	x	x	x
HRBS		x	
QSAR		x	
SAGR survey	x	x	x
STARRS-LS	x	x	x
URI and R-URI	x	x	x
WEO survey	x	x	x
WGRA	x	x	x
Assessment Data Sources			
ARAP		x	x
Azimuth Check		x	
BSH SAT		x	x
Career-Long Assessments: Athena		x	x
Command Assessment Program Peer and Subordinate Assessments		x	x
CSTA		x	x
PDHA and PDHRA		x	
PHA		x	x
Record Data Sources			
AFMES		x	
Army Crime Report	x	x	
ALERTS	x		
BHDP		x	

21

Data Source	Occurrence	Risk Factors	Protective Factors
DAMIS		X	
DHA MODS e-Profile		X	
EEO iComplaints	X		
FASOR		X	
ICRS	X	X	
MFLC data		X	
MEO Database	X		
MJO	X	X	
Platform Data Sources			
Advana	X	X	X
ASMIS 2.0		X	
BSHOP RFI Database		X	
CRRT	X	X	X
DEOCS Commanders Dashboard	X	X	X
DMED		X	
DMSS		X	
JARVISS		X	
LE D-DEx		X	
MDR		X	
M2		X	
OSIE DEOCS	X	X	X
OSIE Resilience Index	X	X	X
PDE	X	X	X
SMS drug testing		X	
SMS SHARP	X	X	

According to our SMEs, the main data source for tracking cases of sexual assault is DSAID. DSAID is DoD's official data source for tracking and maintaining information on sexual assault cases for all members of the armed forces. DSAID tracks sexual assaults committed by or against service members, including retaliation allegations related to unrestricted reports (DoD, 2016). This information is entered through a specific standardized form. However, access to this database is limited to sexual assault response coordinators, Office of the Judge Advocate General personnel, and program managers at more-senior levels, and they have access only to cases within their area of responsibility. A 2022 GAO report found that roughly 89 percent of SHARP personnel do not have access to DSAID, which likely results in underreporting of sexual assaults.

The main Army data source for tracking sexual harassment complaints is the ICRS. It tracks informal, formal, and anonymous complaints of sexual harassment, including data on sexual harassment retaliation. The EEO iComplaints database also tracks complaints of sexual harassment for civilian members and includes cases in which the alleged perpetrator was an active-duty member.

To help integrate data, the Army also maintains the SHARP dashboard, populated with data from DSAID and ICRS, to track incidents. This dashboard displays the number of incidents by period, report date, gender, age, rank, and location, as well as the case management workload of SHARP staff. Additional information on sexual assaults and official sexual harassment complaints made or escalated to law enforcement agencies in the Army might also be available in law enforcement agency data sources (e.g., ALERTS, JARVISS).

Experts recommend that self-reported anonymous or confidential surveys should be used to capture more-accurate prevalence estimates of sexual assault and sexual harassment, much like they recommend for other harmful behaviors (Acosta, Chinman, and Shearer, 2021). This is because undercounts of reported incidents mask the true prevalence of sexual assault and harassment due to various barriers to reporting, such as a culture of shame around experiencing assault, victim-blaming, and posttraumatic stress from the incident (Sadler et al., 2021). For DoD, the WGRA is considered the official data source for estimating the prevalence of sexual assault (i.e., unwanted sexual contact) and sexual harassment (National Defense Research Institute, 2014). A similar survey, the SAGR survey, is also used for prevalence estimates of unwanted sexual contact at the service academies. In our interviews, the SMEs highlighted concerns about attempts to use such data sources as DSAID and ICRS to estimate the prevalence of sexual assault instead of these surveys. There are also other surveys, such as the URI and the DEOCS, that include relevant data but focus on the unit or command level.

As discussed in prior sections of this report, although the WGRA is considered the official source for estimating prevalence of these harmful behaviors, the OPA has noted some limitations in tracking trends over time, given recent changes to measures on the survey (GAO, 2022). Our SMEs highlighted changes in survey measures between waves, noting that such shifts can limit the ability to accurately conduct aggregated analyses over time. For example, in 2014, the RAND Military Workplace Study developed scales of sexual assault that were also used in the WGRA between 2016 and 2019, but the 2021 WGRA switched to an alternative five-item scale of unwanted sexual contact (Calkins et al., 2022). Similar changes to measures affect comparisons on the SAGR survey as well.

Tracked risk factors for sexual assault and sexual harassment perpetration and victimization include a toxic or permissive unit climate (e.g., URI, DEOCS), counterproductive leadership behaviors (e.g., Athena and CASAL), the availability and misuse of alcohol (e.g., DAMIS), and harmful gender norms (e.g., WGRA, SAGR survey). Tracked risk factors specific to perpetration include previous incidents of sexual assault or harassment perpetration by the individual and being of the male gender, while tracked risk factors specific to victimization include female gender, young age, low educational attainment, non-heterosexual orientation, combat exposure, and deployment history. Tracked protective factors for both perpetration and victimization include positive unit climate and positive leadership behaviors. Notably, the 2021 WGRA, in addition to being the official source for prevalence estimates of sexual assault and sexual harassment, included measures to assess relevant risk and protective factors, such as workplace hostility, tolerance for harassment, leader and peer efforts to prevent sexual assault, and bystander intervention (DoD, OPA, undated-c). Finally, although DoD and the Army have several data sources related to sexual assault and sexual harassment, the Independent Review Commission on Sexual Assault in the Military found in its review that DoD knows less about perpetration of sexual assault and harassment than about victimization and that DoD lacks sufficient data to inform perpetration reduction efforts and to assess their effectiveness (DoD, 2021).

Substance Use

Data sources containing information on substance use, related risk factors, and related protective factors are listed in Table 6.

Table 6. Data Sources for Substance Use, by Type

Data Source	Occurrence	Risk Factors	Protective Factors
Survey Data Sources			
BH Pulse	X	X	X
CASAL		X	X
DEOCS	X	X	X
HRBS	X	X	X
SAGR survey	X	X	X
STARRS-LS	X	X	X
URI and R-URI	X	X	X
Assessment Data Sources			
ARAP		X	X
Azimuth Check	X	X	
BSH SAT		X	X
Career-Long Assessments: Athena		X	X
Command Assessment Program Peer and Subordinate Assessments		X	X
CSTA		X	X
MRAT		X	
PHA	X	X	X
PDHA and PDHRA	X	X	

Data Source	Occurrence	Risk Factors	Protective Factors
Record Data Sources			
AFMES	x	x	
Army Crime Report	x	x	
ALERTS	x	x	
BHDP	x	x	x
DAMIS	x	x	x
DCIPS	x		
DHA MODS e-Profile	x	x	
FASOR	x	x	
MFLC data	x	x	
MJO	x	x	
Platform Data Sources			
Advana	x	x	x
ASMIS 2.0	x	x	
BSHOP RFI Database	x	x	
CRRT	x	x	x
DEOCS Commanders Dashboard	x	x	x
DMED		x	
DMSS	x	x	
JARVISS	x	x	
LE D-DEx	x	x	
MDR	x	x	x
M2	x	x	x
OSIE DEOCS	x	x	x
OSIE Resilience Index	x	x	x
PDE	x	x	x
SMS drug testing	x	x	

Our definition of substance use comprises hazardous alcohol use, the use of prescription medications either without a prescription or more than prescribed, and the use of illegal drugs.[19] Data

---

[19] More detail on this definition is available in Appendix A.

on hazardous alcohol use include self-reported use on surveys, such as the URI and HRBS; assessments, such as the PHA, which uses the AUDIT-C scoring system to identify individuals for counseling and referral for evaluation; and DAMIS, which tracks the treatment, counseling, and rehabilitation of Army Substance Abuse Program (ASAP) participants. Data on the use of illegal drugs or misuse of prescription medications include drug testing data (e.g., SMS drug testing); self-reported use on surveys, such as URI and HRBS; and information on drug-related ASAP activities in DAMIS. Additionally, information on any type of substance use might be available in law enforcement agency records (e.g., ALERTS) and safety monitoring data (e.g., ASMIS 2.0) when substance use is documented as an underlying cause or contributing factor of a violation or incident tracked in these data. Finally, substance use might be indicated in medical or health records, such as MDR records, when the individual either voluntarily sought care or experienced a medical issue related to substance use that required treatment.

The completeness of substance use data sources depends on factors unique to each type of data. Drug testing data will include information only on tested substances that an individual used recently enough, and in sufficient quantity, to be detectable. Because drug testing is mandatory for all Army personnel, the individuals tested are randomly selected on a monthly basis, and drug tests occur quickly enough after random assignment that the individual cannot anticipate and defer substance use until after the test, these data are suitable for estimating the prevalence of substance use for the *tested* substances (Army Regulation 600-85, 2020).

Medical records will include information on substance use only for individuals who received care, either through voluntary self-referral or because they experienced an adverse medical event that required treatment. One SME noted that, although medical records are the best source of alcohol and substance use disorder diagnoses, these records might not contain information on harmful behaviors related to substance use, such as accidents that occurred while an individual was under the influence of a substance. This is because the role of substance use in the medical encounter is not always reported. Additionally, although more-detailed information exists in the form of "profiles" written by the medical provider, these profiles are protected health information and cannot be accessed or used outside a clinical context.[20] However, information derived from these profiles might be available to commanders through the e-Profile database if it pertains to the deployability of a soldier in their unit.

Finally, surveys and health assessments, such as PHA, will include only information on substance use that the individual voluntarily self-reported. Individuals might be more likely to self-report the use of substances, especially for sensitive topics like illicit drug use, on anonymous surveys than on surveys where responses are linked to individual identities (Durant, Cary, and Schroder, 2002; Singer, Von Thurn, and Miller, 1995). Some surveys that ask about substance use (e.g., URI, HRBS) also ask about its effects on the individual's life, such as difficulty performing duties at work. Because the Army does not test for alcohol use, surveys that can be weighted to derive estimates representative of the entire Army, such as the HRBS, are most appropriate for estimating the prevalence of general alcohol use and alcohol use disorders. However, the possibility that individuals might underreport their frequency or intensity of alcohol use might result in underestimated prevalence. Additionally, health assessments performed periodically (e.g., PHA), before deployment (e.g., PHRA), and after

---

[20] In some cases, the Army or DoD sponsor projects that provide access to researchers outside of the Army or DoD, but this only occurs in specific circumstances with explicit approval by the sponsoring agency.

deployment (e.g., PDHRA) can be used for screening and early identification of alcohol use disorders and to refer individuals for further evaluation.

Major risk factors for substance use tracked in our data sources include past occurrences of substance use, demographics (e.g., low educational attainment, male gender, young age), combat exposure, deployment history, and toxic or permissive unit climate. Law enforcement agency data, such as JARVISS, might also contain information on the availability of illegal drugs on or near Army bases via georeferenced information on drug trafficking cases. Tracked protective factors include unit cohesion, positive leadership engagement, and spirituality.

Of the harmful behaviors included in this study, information on substance use is included in the largest number of available data sources. The information on alcohol use—which is both a harmful behavior and a known risk factor of suicide, use of other substances, domestic abuse, and sexual assault or harassment—is generally more detailed and appears in more data sources than information on illegal substance use and the misuse of prescription medications. Among our data sources, the HRBS contains the most detailed self-reported information on illegal use of such substances as marijuana, cocaine, and prescription drugs without a prescription or in greater amounts, more often, or for longer than prescribed. More broadly, the ability to combine self-reported data from surveys and health assessments, surveillance testing data, and the records of medical services and law enforcement agencies enables a more complete picture of substance use in the Army because the unique advantages of these respective types of data complement each other. Furthermore, although there is integration of data on substance use incidents and prevention activities through DAMIS, our SMEs noted that DAMIS is an older system that was not designed to conduct these analyses and might be difficult to use. Easier-to-use data derived from DAMIS on behaviors, risks, and prevention activities are available to commanders through the CRRT. The SMS drug testing dashboard is also intended to provide more–readily available information.

Substance use requires an integrated prevention approach because, in addition to being a risk factor for other harmful behaviors, it is frequently comorbid with other risk factors, such as mental health conditions. According to the Substance Abuse and Mental Health Services Association (2022), about 44 percent of adults 18 or older who had a substance use disorder in 2021 also had a mental illness in the same year. This introduces a challenge because the prevention activities best suited to prevent a co-occurring substance use disorder and mental illness might differ, depending on which condition occurred first. To determine this in a broader context, it is necessary to have frequent, consistent, and quick turnaround surveys screening the same individual over time for both substance use behaviors and poor mental health. Although multiple surveys we identified, such as the HRBS, ask about both substance use behaviors and mental health status, these surveys are not intended to screen individuals for rapid-response activities. However, the structure of the BH Pulse survey, which is designed for quick analyses of public health concerns identified by behavioral health officers or commanders, might be suitable for this purpose if the surveys are administered frequently enough. However, these surveys are still intended to provide results at an aggregated unit level, not for individual soldier screening or intervention. Additionally, the PHA and related PHRA and the PDHRA are designed to screen individuals for hazardous alcohol use based on the AUDIT-C scoring system and refer them for additional evaluation; however, these assessments take place annually or upon deployment status changes and thus might not capture harmful behaviors or risk factors for up to a year after their initiation.

Suicide

Data sources containing information on suicide, related risk factors, and related protective factors for suicide are listed in Table 7.

Table 7. Data Sources for Suicide, by Type

Data Source	Occurrence	Risk Factors	Protective Factors
Survey Data Sources			
Active-Duty Spouse Survey		x	x
BH Pulse	x	x	x
CASAL		x	x
DEOCS		x	x
HRBS	x	x	x
SAGR survey		x	x
SOFS	x	x	x
STARRS-LS	x	x	x
URI and R-URI	x	x	x
Assessment Data Sources			
ARAP		x	x
Azimuth Check		x	x
BSH SAT		x	x
CSTA		x	x
MRAT		x	
PHA	x	x	
PDHA and PDHRA		x	
Record Data Sources			
AFMES	x	x	
Army Crime Report	x	x	
ALERTS	x		
BHDP	x	x	x
DCIPS	x		

28

Data Source	Occurrence	Risk Factors	Protective Factors
DHA MODS e-Profile	x	x	
DoDSER	x	x	
DAMIS		x	
FASOR		x	
MFLC data		x	
MJO		x	
Platform Data Sources			
Advana	x	x	x
ASMIS 2.0		x	
BSHOP RFI Database	x	x	x
CRRT	x	x	x
DEOCS Commanders Dashboard		x	x
DMED		x	
DMSS	x	x	
JARVISS	x	x	
LE D-DEx	x	x	
MDR	x	x	x
M2	x	x	x
OSIE DEOCS		x	x
OSIE Resilience Index	x	x	x
PDE	x	x	x
SMS ASPP	x		
SMS drug testing		x	

Data on suicide fall into three main categories: suicidal ideation, suicide attempts, and records of deaths from suicide. For deaths from suicide (confirmed and suspected), the authoritative source for determining counts and rates for active-duty service members across DoD is the AFMES, which is responsible for making an official determination on manner (i.e., natural, accident, suicide, homicide, undetermined, or pending), and cause of death (e.g., firearms, hanging). The Defense Suicide Prevention Office produces quarterly and annual reports of suicide counts and rates based on the AFMES. Services are also required to complete a DoDSER for all suicide deaths and attempts. Data on suicide deaths can also be found in several other data sources, such as the DCIPS, which tracks any manner of death, and the casualty death file in the MDR. Data can also be found in other incident reports from medical care providers (e.g., the BHDP) or law enforcement agencies (e.g., ALERTS). However, these data sources might capture only those deaths that are encountered by behavioral health providers or members of law enforcement and might not be updated as medical examiners and coroners gather evidence to change undetermined manners of death to suicides. Based on our interviews with SMEs and review of the documented data sources, we find that the Army has clear and robust systems in place to track known deaths from suicide. However, our SMEs noted that the accuracy of the data is only as good as the judgment of medical providers or local coroners when determining whether a death is a suicide, which reflects a global challenge associated with determining manner of death (Stone et al., 2017).

Data on suicide attempts are available from the same incident report sources described above and from self-reported incidents on some surveys (e.g., URI, HRBS, SOFS). These surveys also include questions pertinent to suicidal ideation (i.e., thoughts of suicide, planning to attempt suicide). Data on suicide attempts and ideation have additional limitations. Our SMEs raised particular concerns that data on reported suicide attempts might be incomplete. Primarily, this is because suicide attempts often go underreported. In addition, one SME noted that because the same form is used to record both deaths from suicide and suicide attempts in DoDSER, many providers fail to fill out the form for attempts because it seems more tailored to deaths. Surveys on suicide attempts and ideation that are designed to provide population estimates of prevalence (e.g., HRBS) provide a better source of data in these cases.

In terms of risk and protective factors, our SMEs indicated that, although they felt they have access to key individual-level risk and protective factors, there was a gap in understanding and monitoring higher-level community and environmental factors. Risk factors for suicide tracked in our data sources include poor mental health, alcohol misuse, and demographic information (e.g., male gender, low educational attainment, race, ethnicity). Protective factors tracked include marital status, spirituality, and information related to unit and command climate, such as cohesiveness and positive leadership behaviors. However, factors related to health status and unhealthy behaviors (e.g., poor mental health, substance misuse) and those related to organizational climate (e.g., unit cohesion, counterproductive leadership behaviors) are found in different data sources, which might be a barrier to holistic assessment of an individual's risk. We also note that, although the data sources we identified contain information about some known risk and protective factors of suicide, not all data sources are necessarily appropriate for ascertaining or confirming whether a particular characteristic or behavior is a risk or protective factor. DoDSER, a key source of suicide-related data for the Army and all other DoD service branches, explicitly cautions against using the data for identifying risk and protective factors because these data do not necessarily contain a representative sample of suicide attempts. Additionally, because DoDSER tracks cases without a comparison group, "risk" is impossible to measure. The BSH SAT contains many of the key factors noted above, but this is done by request only and is intended to provide unit-level results at this time.

Despite these gaps and limitations, unlike some of the other harmful behaviors in this review, the Army has been leading the way in collecting and analyzing data on suicide risk and protective factors through the Army Study to Assess Risk and Resilience in Service Members (STARRS) project, which began in 2009 (see Kessler et al., 2013) and was extended and expanded in 2015 as the STARRS-LS. In a report on preventing suicide in the U.S. military, a congressionally appointed

Independent Review Committee noted the value of this research data and the potential for it to accelerate researchers' ability to understand suicide in the military (Suicide Prevention and Response Independent Review Committee, 2023).

Additional Notes on Harmful Behavior, Risk Factor, and Protective Factor Coverage

Users of data pertaining to harmful behaviors in the Army might prefer sources that simultaneously contain information about a harmful behavior and its risk or protective factors, or information about multiple harmful behaviors. We find that a majority of data sources in our repository contain information of some kind on two or more harmful behaviors simultaneously. A little more than one-half contain information about reports of a harmful behavior *and* information about risk factors or protective factors for the same harmful behavior simultaneously. The most complete, holistic picture of harmful behaviors and their risk and protective factors is available through platforms and dashboards, such as the CRRT, which currently contains at least some information on every harmful behavior within the scope of this report and continues to integrate additional data. There are also other non-platform sources of information, such as the URI, that contain data on multiple harmful behaviors and their risk and protective factors. However, it is important to note the URI is completely anonymous and cannot be used for individually targeted prevention activities. The URI is also designed to assess risks only at the unit level, provides unweighted results, and is not intended for Army-wide prevalence estimates of any given risk factor.

Many risk and protective factors in the study that guided our data identification are shared across harmful behaviors (see Wolters et al., 2023). As a result, data sources that feature information on a particular risk or protective factor might be able to be used for risk analyses of multiple harmful behaviors. Additionally, some of the harmful behaviors reviewed for this study are themselves risk factors for other harmful behaviors, such as substance use (more specifically, alcohol misuse) being a known risk factor for suicide, use of other substances, domestic abuse, and sexual assault or harassment. In general, among the data sources we identified, the most-covered risk and protective factors include previous engagement in the harmful behavior, demographic information (e.g., gender, race, ethnicity, rank), and unit climate factors (e.g., an individual's comfort with reporting harmful behavior incidents to their commander). Less information is available on the individual perceptions, norms, and attitudes that might contribute to harmful behavior risks. Additionally, less information is available and known regarding broader community-oriented or environmental factors. The model we used for our assessment identified fewer risk factors related to unit, installation, local community, or the Army overall (see Wolters et al., 2023). Data are also lacking on protective factors.

Finally, as noted earlier in the report, our review indicates whether a data source contains some information on risk or protective factors as defined in the framework from Wolters et al. (2023). However, in many cases, the validity and reliability of a particular measure of that risk or protective factor, including whether it is related to a particular harmful behavior, might still need to be assessed.

Summary of Findings, Key Gaps, and Recommendations

This project identified a total of 54 data sources relevant to the Army that contain information on domestic abuse, prohibited discrimination, sexual assault and sexual harassment, substance use, and suicide. These sources include data on incidents or cases involving these behaviors as well as anonymous or confidential surveys that can be used to estimate prevalence. We also identified data sources that contain information on risk and protective factors related to these harmful behaviors.

In the following sections, we summarize our key findings related to the data sources we identified, noting any limitations or gaps in their ability to be used for prevention efforts. We then present our recommendations for actions that the Army can take to help address these limitations and gaps to help build a more robust system of data that can support the prevention of harmful behaviors.

Data Sources on the Occurrence of Harmful Behaviors

In our review of data sources on the occurrence of the harmful behaviors focused on for this study, we found the following:

- The Army has data systems for tracking reports of harmful behaviors, but the accuracy of these systems can be limited for a variety of reasons (e.g., barriers to reporting for victims, limitations on who can access these databases and input data, limited or poor training around categorization of certain harmful behaviors such as suicide or domestic abuse).
- Data on the occurrence of these harmful behaviors are often tracked in multiple different data sources, which are owned by a myriad of different organizations. This limits the use of these data in obtaining a more comprehensive picture of the occurrence of these harmful behaviors and the extent to which they might co-occur.
- Given concerns regarding underreporting, DoD has developed anonymous and confidential surveys to better estimate the true prevalence of certain harmful behaviors. Our SMEs noted that there can be limitations with some of these surveys; there are concerns about the small response rates to some of these surveys, changes in measures that limit the ability to track trends over time, and surveys' ability to provide insight into prevalence at smaller organizational levels of analysis. The limited frequency of these surveys and the lag times between data collection and the publication of results might also limit the suitability of these survey data for quick-response prevention efforts. In addition, at the time of this study, there was a gap in being able to provide more-accurate prevalence estimates around domestic abuse in the Army or DoD.
- Our SMEs raised concerns that at local levels, there is a lack of knowledge of and access to the best data sources for estimating prevalence. Instead, personnel rely on whatever data sources are accessible, often without understanding their limitations.

Recommendations

To address these gaps, we recommend that the Army

- look for ways to facilitate better data sharing and integration across harmful behaviors to provide a more comprehensive picture of harmful behaviors[21]
- explore ways to modify or build on existing data collection efforts to make more-frequent and more-recent survey data on harmful behavior occurrences available, such as administering minimal pared-down versions of existing surveys or "pulse surveys" on a more regular basis (e.g., monthly) alongside full survey efforts[22]
- advocate that DoD incorporate a measure of domestic abuse into its confidential surveys that are already designed to assess prevalence of other harmful behaviors
- ensure that personnel involved in prevention of harmful behaviors receive information and guidance on available data sources that measure the prevalence of harmful behaviors, including which data sources are the most appropriate for certain purposes and any limitations to their use, focusing particularly on taking a public health surveillance approach to facilitate primary prevention as outlined in the PPoA 2.0.

As noted in a prior section of the report, our SMEs commented that personnel do not always have access to the proper databases for inputting incidents or might not be accurately recording incidents, which leads to further underreporting. It was beyond the scope of this study to validate or investigate these concerns, but future research might want to explore the extent to which this is an issue.

Data Collection on Risk and Protective Factors

In our review of data sources on risk and protective factors of harmful behaviors, we found the following:

- Data are collected on numerous individual-level factors, but the data are often located across different databases and not easily accessible for use in harmful behavior prevention. The prevention workforce and others seeking relevant information on risk and protective factors might not be permitted to access the databases that house it. (See the "Data Access Issues" section below for more details.)
- Although numerous individual-level risk factors have been identified and are tracked in data sources, we found less information about broader community-oriented or environmental factors. The framework from Wolters et al. (2023) that we used for our study identified few risk factors related to unit, installation, local community, or the Army overall, which suggests a need for more research on these factors.
- Despite numerous risk factors being tracked (with the limitations noted above), data are lacking on protective factors. Fewer protective factors were identified in Wolters et al. (2023), and fewer data sources collect information on protective factors.

---

[21] At the time of this study, the Army was already forming an integrated data working group that should be able to help build a foundation for this recommendation.

[22] Such "pulse survey" efforts would have to be balanced with potential survey fatigue. The Army would need to ensure that these surveys are kept very short and involve minimal time for the participant.

- Even though risk and protective factors do address both victimization and perpetration for harmful behaviors that involve more than one actor, our SMEs noted that related prevention and data collection efforts are by nature victim-centric rather than perpetrator-centric. As noted earlier, the Independent Review Commission on Sexual Assault in the Military also commented on DoD's inability to make evidence-based decisions to reduce perpetration (DoD, 2021).
- Data on risk and protective factors and occurrences of harmful behaviors are often collected in separate data sources, which makes it difficult to make connections between the two categories of data.

Recommendations

To address these gaps, we recommend that the Army

- continue to research community-based and environmental risk factors and identify relevant data that might already be collected for integration into prevention efforts as warranted
- continue to conduct research to identify potential protective factors for harmful behaviors and integrate relevant existing data into prevention efforts
- explore ways to better understand and collect data around risks for perpetration
- integrate relevant data sources and ensure appropriate access to these sources, so that the prevention workforce and others supporting prevention efforts can connect data on risk and protective factors with data on occurrence of harmful behaviors, which should include leveraging aggregate-level data to facilitate a more population-level and public health approach when implementing primary prevention.

Ability to Analyze Relevant Data

In our review of data sources on harmful behaviors, we also explored the ability to analyze data in support of integrated primary prevention, such as the ability to look at trends within certain demographic groups or organizational units. as well as conducting longitudinal analyses to identify trends over time. We found the following:

- Although many data sources include demographic variables as part of their data collection, they might not be collected in a standardized manner. Specifically, categorizations of race and ethnicity can differ, which limits these types of comparisons across data sources or even within merged datasets. Notably, the Independent Review Commission on Sexual Assault in the Military recommended improved data collection and reporting of the experiences of service members from marginalized populations, including racial and ethnic minorities (DoD, 2021). To address this recommendation and ensure that trends by race and ethnicity related to harmful behaviors are attainable, racial and ethnic comparisons are necessary.
- Organizational data, such as unit or command identification, are often not included in the data sources relevant to harmful behavior prevention or might not be standardized across years or data sources. This significantly limits analysis of harmful behaviors at this level, unless the data source can be linked to other data sources that include the relevant organizational

data. This effort, however, requires intensive resources, advanced skillsets to merge datasets, and access to individual-level data with person identifiers. Being able to review data and track trends at the installation and command levels is critical for commanders, for primary prevention efforts at the local level, and for evaluating the effectiveness of those prevention efforts.

- The ability to conduct longitudinal analyses can be limited by changes in data collection procedures and the extent to which individuals can be tracked over time. Similarly, although some surveys are designed to facilitate longitudinal comparisons, our SMEs noted that measures on some surveys, such as the DEOCS and WGRA, have changed over time, which limits comparisons. Other surveys can also be limited due to different sampling frames or response rates.

- Our review indicates whether a data source contains information identified as being a risk or protective factor, but the validity and reliability of the particular measure of that risk or protective factor, including whether it is related to a particular harmful behavior, might still need to be assessed in many cases.

Recommendations

To address these gaps, we recommend that the Army

- standardize racial and ethnic categories across data sources to enable analysis by race and ethnicity
- include organizational-level identifiers in data sources relevant to harmful behavior prevention where possible, without raising confidentiality issues, to enable analysis at different organizational levels
- ensure that survey measures of harmful behaviors and risk and protective factors have been analyzed to assess their reliability and validity, and that those critical measures that have been validated and found reliable are maintained over time to facilitate longitudinal analyses
- ensure that prevention personnel understand potential data limitations to being able to make comparisons over time so that they draw accurate conclusions from available data
- explore ways to facilitate better longitudinal analyses on key variables relevant to prevention of harmful behaviors.

Data Access Issues

In our review of data sources on harmful behaviors, we also explored the extent to which data were accessible for use by individuals outside the office of primary responsibility. We found the following:

- The permissions required to access data vary by type of data, and many data sources feature tiers of access available to different individuals, depending on their credentials and intended use for the data.

- There is a lack of knowledge about which data sources are available and how to access key sources of data. As noted earlier, this issue can lead to individuals using whatever data sources are accessible to them, regardless of whether it is the best source of data for their purposes.
- Due to concerns around privacy, potential identifiability of participants, and potential misinterpretations of data, many organizations keep data under a very close hold and are willing to release only aggregate-level data, if they release any at all. Our SMEs noted this data access issue presents a barrier to true integrated prevention because efforts end up being siloed and potential valuable sources of data, particularly on risk and protective factors, are not shared.

Recommendations

To address these gaps, we recommend that the Army

- explore approaches for sharing and integrating data in ways that help address concerns around data sensitivity, but still provide access and information to key stakeholder groups[23]
- leverage the work from this project to maintain a list of key data sources that includes documentation of who can be granted access to different data sources, what type of access can be granted, and what the process is for receiving access permission
- leverage working groups, such as the Army integrated data working group, to facilitate better access and data sharing where appropriate.[24]

Conclusion

This study identifies a multitude of different data sources that contain information on harmful behaviors, their risk factors, and their protective factors. Although there are challenges and limitations in using many of these data sources, identifying their existence is the first step in being able to develop more-effective approaches to integrated primary prevention. This report provides recommendations for addressing some of these barriers by refining current data collection efforts through a better understanding of relevant risk and protective factors, better integration of data sources to make them more useful, and improved access to data for the prevention workforce and others who are involved in harmful behavior prevention efforts. Importantly, our recommendations emphasize this need for improved data collection refinement, integration, and access, rather than suggesting the Army undertake significant additional data collection efforts. Additionally, although it was outside the scope of the study to assess Army prevention efforts, it is critical for the Army to explore ways that data can support assessing the effectiveness of these efforts. Finally, this study focused on identifying data sources that contain information on risk and protective factors that is important for primary

---

[23] The Army has already taken some significant steps in this direction through the development of various dashboards. For example, the CRRT provides commanders with key risk data from multiple data sources that are critical for prevention efforts while still protecting the sensitivity of individual data. DoD is also creating its own dashboards, such as the OSIE Risk Index in Advana, to pull multiple data sources into one platform.

[24] As noted earlier in the report, at the time of this study, the Army recently formed an integrated data working group focused on harmful behaviors that should be able to help build a foundation for this recommendation.

prevention of harmful behaviors. To provide a comprehensive public health approach to prevention, future work should also include data relevant to secondary and tertiary prevention.

Glossary of Harmful Behaviors

This appendix contains more-detailed definitions from official DoD policy for each of the harmful behaviors included in this study.

Domestic abuse: "Domestic violence, or a pattern of behavior resulting in emotional or psychological abuse, economic control, or interference with personal liberty that is directed toward a person who is a: current or former spouse; person with whom the alleged abuser shares a child in common; current or former intimate partner with whom the alleged abuser shares or has shared a common domicile; or person who is or has been in a social relationship of a romantic or intimate nature with the accused and determined to be an intimate partner" (DoDI 6400.06, 2023, p. 80).

Prohibited discrimination: "Discrimination, including disparate treatment, of an individual or group on the basis of race, color, national origin, religion, sex (including pregnancy), gender identity, or sexual orientation that is not otherwise authorized by law or regulation and detracts from military readiness" (DoDI 1350.02, 2022, p. 38).

Sexual assault: "Intentional sexual contact characterized by the use of force, threats, intimidation, or abuse of authority or when the victim does not or cannot consent. As used in this Instruction, the term includes a broad category of sexual offenses consisting of the following specific UCMJ [Uniform Code of Military Justice] offenses: rape, sexual assault, aggravated sexual contact, abusive sexual contact, forcible sodomy (forced oral or anal sex), or attempts to commit these offenses" (DoDI 6495.02, Volume 1, 2013, p. 137).

Sexual harassment: "Conduct that:

- Involves unwelcome sexual advances, requests for sexual favors, and deliberate or repeated offensive comments or gestures of a sexual nature when:

    - Submission to such conduct is, either explicitly or implicitly, made a term or condition of a person's job, pay, or career;
    - Submission to or rejection of such conduct by a person is used as a basis for career or employment decisions affecting that person; or
    - Such conduct has the purpose or effect of unreasonably interfering with an individual's work performance or creates an intimidating, hostile, or offensive working environment.

- Is so severe or pervasive that a reasonable person would perceive, and the victim does perceive, the environment as hostile or offensive.

- Any use or condonation, by any person in a supervisory or command position, of any form of sexual behavior to control, influence, or affect the career, pay, or job of a member of the Armed Forces or a civilian employee of the Department of Defense.

- Any deliberate or repeated unwelcome verbal comments or gesture of a sexual nature by any member of the Armed Forces or a civilian employee of the Department of Defense.

There is no requirement for concrete psychological harm to the complainant for behavior to constitute sexual harassment. Behavior is sufficient to constitute sexual harassment if it is so severe or pervasive that a reasonable person would perceive, and the complainant does perceive, the environment as hostile or offensive.

Sexual harassment can occur through electronic communications, including social media, other forms of communication, and in person" (DoDI 1020.03, 2022, p. 22).

Substance use: DoDI 1010.04 defines *problematic substance use, substance or drug misuse,* and *at-risk or hazardous alcohol use* separately. For the purposes of this study, we considered all three of these definitions as included in the scope of *substance use*:

- **At-risk or hazardous alcohol use:** "The consumption of alcohol in daily or weekly amounts greater than those defined as safe by the U.S. Preventive Task Force. Drinking at levels above the recommended amounts places an individual at greater risk for illness, injury, or social or legal problems" (DoDI 1010.14, 2014, p. 26).
- **Problematic substance use:** "The use of any substance in a manner that puts the user at risk of failing in their responsibilities to mission or family, or that is considered unlawful by regulation, policy, or law. This includes substance use that results in negative consequences to the health and/or well-being of the user or others; or meets the criteria for an SUD [substance use disorder]" (DoDI 1010.14, 2014, p. 28).
- **Substance or drug misuse:** "The use of any substance with or without a prescription with the primary goal to alter one's mental state (i.e., to alter mood, emotion, or state of consciousness) outside of its medically prescribed purpose. May include medications, illicit drugs, or use of a commercial product outside its intended purpose (such as inhalants or synthetic cannabinoids)" (DoDI 1010.14, 2014, p. 28).

Suicide: "Death caused by self-directed injurious behavior with an intent to die as a result of the behavior" (DoDI 6490.16, 2023, p. 38).

- **Suicidal ideation:** "Thinking about, considering, or planning suicide" (DoDI 6490.16, 2023, p. 38).
- **Suicide attempt:** "A non-fatal, self-directed, potentially injurious behavior with an intent to die as a result of the behavior" (DoDI 6490.16, 2023, p. 38).

Risk and Protective Factors Identified by Wolters et al. (2023)

Wolters et al. (2023) took a multipronged approach to develop a map of risk and protective factors for harmful behaviors across an Army-specific SEM. The authors started by conducting a comprehensive review of existing reports, peer-reviewed literature, military literature, and government reports using search terms for key harmful behaviors identified by their partners in what was known as the Army Resilience Directorate and is now called the Army Directorate of Prevention Resilience and Readiness. These harmful behaviors were suicide, substance misuse, domestic violence, sexual harassment and assault, discrimination, and extremism. Because our study does not focus on extremism, we do not present the results from Wolters et al. (2023) for this item.

Wolters et al. (2023) developed definitions for each behavior based on DoD definitions (when available) and the civilian prevention literature (for more about those definitions, see Wolters et al., 2023, pg. 5). The Army-specific SEM was developed by reviewing the literature about the risk and protective factors for the harmful behaviors outlined above and qualitatively iterating to combine factors and define socioecological levels where different factors emerged. Figure B.1 presents the Army-specific SEM developed during this process.

Figure B.1. Army-Specific Social-Ecological Model

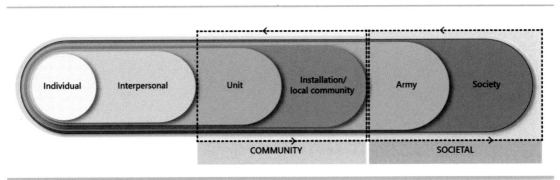

SOURCE: Reproduced from Wolters et al. (2023).

The review by Wolters et al. (2023) of the literature identified and substantiated 40 crosscutting risk factors and 15 crosscutting protective factors for the harmful behaviors, which are presented in Tables B.1 and B.2. A "P" indicates that the factor is a risk factor for "perpetrating" the harmful behavior in that column. Conversely, a "V" indicates that there is research to suggest that the factor is a risk factor for "victimization." By extension, "VP" indicates that the factor puts a person at higher risk for both victimization *and* perpetration. Some harmful behaviors do not have a victim or perpetrator, and those risk factors do not have any qualifying indicator. Although we do not present it here, Wolters et al. (2023) also highlight in their report the key individual risk and protective factors for each harmful behavior because not all risk and protective factors are crosscutting.

Table B.1. Crosscutting Risk Factors Across the Army-Specific Social-Ecological Model

Factor	Suicide	Substance Use	Domestic Violence	Sexual Assault or Harassment	Discrimination
Individual-Level Factors					
Gender: male	x	x	P	P	P
Poor mental health	x	x	VP	VP	V
Marital status: unmarried	x	x	V	V	V
Age: young adult	x	x	VP	V	P
Low education attainment	x	x	VP	V	P
Financial stress	x	x	VP		V
Rank: enlisted	x	x	VP	VP	P
Antisocial and aggressive behavior	x	x	P	P	
Impulsivity	x	x	P	P	
Past exposure to trauma or abuse	x	x	VP	VP	
Alcohol misuse	x	x	VP	VP	
Unhealthy or dysfunctional parenting		x	P	VP	
Deployment		x	VP	V	
Non-heterosexual orientation	x			V	V
Gender: female			V	V	V
Lower rank: junior enlisted or junior officer	x	x		V	
Combat exposure	x	x		V	
Hostile gender attitudes and beliefs			P	P	P
Previously committed the harmful behavior	x	x		P	
Low SES			VP	V	
Race and ethnicity: Non-Hispanic White	x	x			

Factor	Suicide	Substance Use	Domestic Violence	Sexual Assault or Harassment	Discrimination
Combat arms occupation	x	x			
Sexual identity crisis	x				V
Poor physical health or recent medical issue	x	x			
Low self-esteem			P		V
Interpersonal-Level Factors					
Association with unhealthy dysfunctional peer groups		x	VP	P	P
Isolation or lack of social support	x		VP	VP	
Close-relationship stressors	x	x	P	P	
Unit-Level Factors					
Stigma associated with reporting and seeking help	x	x	VP	VP	
Toxic or permissive unit climate	x	x		VP	VP
Toxic, ineffective, or weak leadership				VP	VP
Installation- and Local Community–Level Factors					
Availability of alcohol		x	VP	VP	
Access to location or methods	x	x		VP	
Social or community disorganization			VP	VP	
Low community SES			VP		VP
Army-Level Factors					
Stigma associated with reporting and seeking help	x	x	VP	VP	
Harmful norms (e.g., regarding gender, violence, drinking)		x	VP	VP	VP
Structural barriers to accessing help or resolution	x			VP	VP
Society-Level Factors					
Weak policy and law	x	x	VP		VP
Weak economic conditions	x	x	VP		VP

SOURCE: Adapted from Wolters et al. (2023).
NOTE: x = crosscutting factor; P = the factor is a risk factor for perpetrating the harmful behavior in the column; V = the factor is a risk factor for victimization; VP = the factor puts a person at higher risk for both victimization and perpetration; SES = socioeconomic status.

Table B.2. Crosscutting Protective Factors Across the Army-Specific Social-Ecological Model

Factor	Suicide	Substance Use	Domestic Violence	Sexual Assault or Harassment	Discrimination
Individual-Level Factors					
Life skill: decisionmaking and problem-solving	x	x	P	P	
Life skill: empathy		x	P	P	x
High academic achievement		x	P	P	x
Positive affect	x	x			
Marital status: married	x	x			
Spiritual or religiosity	x	x			
Interpersonal-Level Factors					
Social connectedness and support	x	x	VP	P	
Family cohesion and support	x	x	VP	VP	
Healthy peer relationships		x	P	V	
Unit-Level Factors					
Unit cohesion and connectedness	x	x		VP	VP
Positive leadership and engagement	x	x		VP	VP
Unit-level policy enforcement		x		VP	VP
Installation- and Local Community–Level Factors					
Restrict or limit access to instruments of harmful behavior	x	x	VP		
Community connectedness and support	x		VP		
Army-Level Factors					
Prevention policies		x	VP	VP	VP

SOURCE: Adapted from Wolters et al. (2023).
NOTE: x = crosscutting factor; P = the factor is a risk factor for perpetrating the harmful behavior in the column; V = the factor is a risk factor for victimization; VP = the factor puts a person at higher risk for both victimization and perpetration.

Appendix C

Definition of Key Characteristics Assessed for Each Data Source

This appendix outlines the key data source characteristics that are documented in our data repository.

Core Data Repository Characteristics

Data source name: The name of the data source being documented. For cases in which the data source is frequently referenced as an acronym or an abbreviated name, this abbreviation is written in parentheses after the full name of the data source.

Linked worksheet: A link to more details about the associated data source.

Type of data: The general category of the data source. Values include:

- *Survey:* Any data derived from a survey of an Army or broader DoD population.
- *Assessment:* Regular assessments that might be required for individuals completing curricula (e.g., leadership development) or to monitor certain issues or outcomes of interest (e.g., behavioral health). Unlike surveys, assessments include information about an individual from other people (e.g., peers, supervisors).
- *Record:* An individual's interactions with a particular agency or administrative process reflected in the data (e.g., the person was accused of a violation or had a health issue that required treatment). These interactions might be voluntary (e.g., a doctor's appointment made by an individual to treat an illness) or involuntary (e.g., court-martial, arrest).
- *Platform:* An interface, such as a web portal, that summarizes, visualizes, and aggregates multiple data sources or provides a method for accessing underlying datasets.

Army or DoD level: The organization that owns the data and oversees the sponsor/collecting agency.

Sponsor/collecting agency: The specific agency (e.g., team, directorate, office) responsible for collecting, maintaining, and providing access to the data source.

Occurrence of harmful behavior: Indicator that the data source contains variables or information pertinent to estimating the prevalence or occurrence of reported incidents of a harmful behavior for the population represented in the data.

Risk factors: Indicator that the data source contains variables or information pertinent to estimating the prevalence or occurrence of a known risk factor of a harmful behavior, or to identifying groups of individuals for which the known risk factor applies (e.g., individuals with a history of

44

substance misuse). We define *risk factors* based on previous research for the Army (Wolters et al., 2023).

Protective factors: Indicator that the data source contains variables or information pertinent to estimating the prevalence or occurrence of a known protective factor from a harmful behavior, or identifying groups of individuals for which the known protective factor applies (e.g., units with a positive command climate). We define *protective factors* based on previous research for the Army (Wolters et al., 2023).

Army only: Data source includes data only from the Army and not from any other military service.

Unit of observation: The unit represented by an individual row in the data source. For survey data, this is usually "individual" but might differ for other types of data (e.g., for incident report data, the unit of observation is usually a case). We include the most granular possible unit of observation in the underlying data; in some cases, data might be accessible only at a more aggregated unit of observation (e.g., data that exist at an individual level might be accessible only in the form of aggregated statistics by installation, unless the user has higher-level access permissions).

Component: The duty component within each represented branch of service that is included in the data source: active duty, National Guard, reserve, or civilian.

Longitudinal: An indicator that relevant outcomes for unit(s) of observation can be observed over time in the data source, allowing for the analysis of trends or comparisons between periods within a particular unit.

Time horizon start: The earliest time for which data are available.

Time horizon end: The latest time for which data are available. "Current" means that data are updated on an ongoing basis.

Current frequency: A description of the regular interval at which data are updated at the time of the repository entry. "Real-time" means that data are updated continuously. The frequency at which data are updated might differ from the frequency at which they are made available depending on access permissions.

Aggregate by [variable]: An indicator that the data source allows for analyses comparing certain subgroups to other subgroups based on a certain variable. In some cases, the ability to do aggregate by variable might depend on having access permissions required to observe the relevant grouping variable.

Linked Worksheet Characteristics

Access permissions required: Briefly describes the permissions required to gain access to the data where applicable. This information might include eligibility requirements (e.g., if one must have a common access card or be a member of a particular agency or team to be able to access the data), points of contact to request access permissions, and, where applicable, details on the levels of access permissions required to use different forms of the data (e.g., if summary statistics derived from a data source are publicly available, but direct access to the underlying data requires special permissions).

Notes on units of observation: Additional information about the unit(s) of observation in the data source. This might include information on which types of aggregation are possible, e.g., whether race and ethnicity are available in the data source (with or without special access permissions) to allow the user to re-aggregate the data by racial or ethnic group.

Notes on documentation: Available information about the data documentation, such as the methodology used to create the dataset or codebooks defining the variables contained within the data source. For cases in which the availability of documentation is unclear, this characteristic might include a note on the individual or agency from which documentation can be requested.

Other linkable data sources: List or categorization of other data sources that the user might, either by themselves or by request, merge with the data source using a unique identifier that is shared across data sources.

Notes on data preparation: Any notes on data cleaning processes, special equipment or software, and other requirements to use the data for analyses. This field is most applicable to underlying datasets (also known as *micro-data*) that require the use of statistical software to analyze.

[For survey data] **Notes on survey design:** Information about the design of the survey that populates the dataset, such as survey instruments, sampling frames, and other methodological factors to consider when using the data.

[For survey data] **Notes on weighting:** Where applicable, information about the weights provided with the survey data that can be used to derive representative estimates of the broader population from which the survey was drawn (e.g., a survey of a random sample of active-duty soldiers that can be weighted to represent the entire active-duty population).

Details on harmful behaviors: Information on the harmful behavior(s) tracked in the data source, such as specific definitions of harmful behaviors that apply to that data source, the wording of survey questions, or limitations to consider when using the data to analyze reported incidence of harmful behaviors (e.g., if a data source contains information on only the perpetrator of a harmful behavior and not the victim).

Details on risk or protective factors: Information on the risk or protective factors tracked in the data source. Our classification of risk and protective factors is based on the Army-specific SEM created from a meta-analysis of scientific literature on associations between harmful behavior risk factors and other factors that might increase or decrease this risk (Wolters et al., 2023).

Notes on strengths and limitations: Information on key strengths and limitations of the data source based on SME interviews and RAND analysis. For example, the extent to which a data source can be used to estimate prevalence is based on validated and reliable survey measures and the ability to analyze based on different subgroups, among other criteria.

Harmful Behavior Data Sources and Relevant Personnel Databases Identified in Review

This appendix provides a list and high-level summary for each of the data sources we identified as containing information relevant to measuring incidents or prevalence of the harmful behaviors focused on for this study. This list also includes data sources containing information on relevant harmful behavior risk and protective factors. Table D.1 provides an overview of Army-specific data sources. Table D.2 provides an overview of DoD-level data sources. Finally, Table D.3 provides an overview of key Army personnel databases that contain individual-level demographic information that are common risk factors or protective factors for many of the harmful behaviors in this report.

Unless otherwise cited, the sources for the information in Tables D.1 through D.3 are interviews with our SMEs and briefings that our SMEs provided to us.

Table D.1. High-Level Summary of Army Data Sources

Army Data Source Name	Summary
Army Crime Report	The Army Crime Report is an annual publication by the Office of the Provost Marshal General that aggregates crime statistics among the Army population. The report shows eight-year trends for major categories of crime and illustrative vignettes of crime reports.
Army Law Enforcement Reporting and Tracking System (ALERTS)	ALERTS is the automated reporting system for military law enforcement reporting throughout the Army (Army Regulation 190-45, 2016). The ALERTS database contains information about all Army law enforcement activities, including suspects, victims, the types of offenses, and investigation statuses.
Army Readiness Assessment Program (ARAP)	"ARAP is a Web-based resource that provides battalion-level commanders with data on their formation's readiness posture through seven categories: • **Common Core** - Common Core questions are general and universal questions that are answered by every survey taker. These questions provide a collection of responses utilized to establish a benchmark for the Army's overall safety climate and culture. • **Organizational Processes** - Organizational Processes questions focus on the primary activities that an organization performs to safely and successfully execute its mission. Organizational Processes are things that influence safety daily such as doctrine, regulations, SOP's [standard operating procedures], procedures, training and education, as well as materials and equipment. They directly influence work production effectiveness and efficiency, accident and fatality rates, inspection results, and morale and motivation. • **Organizational Climate** - Organizational Climate questions focus on the Soldiers and/or employees shared perceptions or experiences of the policies, practices, and procedures in their workplace that is associated with expected behaviors that get rewarded and supported. Organizational climate is directly influenced by organizational culture which is a set of shared expectations over time defining appropriate behavior for various situations. • **Resources** - Resources questions focus on whether or not Soldiers and employees collectively view that they are being provided adequate resources throughout the organization to safely complete or perform their assigned task. Resources include things such as personnel, money, time, knowledge/expertise, equipment, safety plans, stress management, and work/ training opportunities. • **Supervision** - Supervision questions evaluate leadership regarding communication, enforcement of written guidance and procedures, and the establishment/implementation/compliance of an organization's safety program. • **Safety Programs** - Safety program questions assess the holistic view of an organization's Safety Program and whether or not it seeks opportunities for improvement that can reduce accident exposure and maximize mission accomplishment. • **Open Ended** - Open-ended questions allow personnel to respond in his/her own words providing specific feedback to the commander regarding their perspective of the organization's safety program, climate and culture" (U.S. Army, undated-a).

Army Data Source Name	Summary
Army Safety Management Information System (ASMIS 2.0)	"ASMIS 2.0, the Army Safety Management Information System 2.0, is a family of information technology systems that underpins the Army Safety and Occupational Health Management System (ASOHMS). It is the first SOH [safety and occupational health] tool to use advanced intelligence to integrate distinct data with a vast array of authoritative systems and data sources across the DOD and other government agencies. It provides a 'one-stop-shop' for all data that is pertinent to Army SOH and presents data and information in an intuitive, leader-centric way that allows the right people to have the right information at the right time to make decisions that impact their organization's safety, risk management and loss prevention efforts" (U.S. Army, undated-b).
Azimuth Check	The Azimuth Check is an updated version of the Global Assessment Tool that equips soldiers with information about their current level of resilience and well-being to promote self-awareness and development. The Azimuth Check is an online, confidential self-assessment survey that takes approximately 12 minutes to complete. The survey assesses a soldier's level of overall fitness across the five dimensions of strength: physical, emotional, social, spiritual, and family. Upon completion of the Azimuth Check, soldiers are provided individualized feedback for each dimension of strength.
Behavioral and Social Health Outcomes Practice Request for Information (BSHOP RFI) Database	The BSHOP RFI database took the place of the Army Behavioral Health Integrated Data Environment (ABHIDE). The ABHIDE contained data from several organizations and was securely stored on a Structured Query Language (SQL) server. During the coronavirus disease 2019 pandemic, BSHOP team members were not able to access the data over the virtual private network. In addition, the Defense Centers for Public Health – Aberdeen personnel did not have the correct statistical software package to connect to the ABHIDE. The team developed a solution that would allow remote access to data, and as a result, the ABHIDE became obsolete and was deleted in September 2022. BSHOP still collects data from many of the original ABHIDE data sources but does not have a data repository. The data that BSHOP receives related to suicidal behavior are now loaded into the BSHOP RFI database. The internal database allows BSHOP to provide quick standardized responses to suicidal behavior inquiries.

"The ABHIDE document[ed] the life of a Soldier with suicidal behavior from accession to discharge or death. It include[d] data on active-duty, activated National Guard, and activated US Army Reserve Soldiers who died by suicide, as identified by the Armed Forces Medical Examiner System, or attempted suicide, experienced suicidal ideation, or inflicted nonsuicidal self-injury, as documented by Department of Defense Suicide Event Reports" (U.S. Army Public Health Center, 2016). |

Army Data Source Name	Summary
Behavioral and Social Health Self-Assessment Tool (BSH SAT)	"A BH EPICON [behavioral health epidemiological consultation] is a public health investigation of a perceived increase in suicidal behavior, aggression, violence, or an associated behavioral or social health issue such as alcohol misuse. The Defense Centers for Public Health – Aberdeen's Division of Behavioral and Social Health Outcomes Practice (BSHOP) designs each BH EPICON to address these public health concerns based on the specific needs of the unit, the commander's intent, and resource and timeline considerations" (U.S. Army Public Health Center, 2017). The BSH SAT is a collaborative instrument between the Defense Centers for Public Health – Aberdeen's BSHOP and the unit's command and staff to systematically identify behavioral or social health concerns and issues facing service members at all levels, and to identify available garrison, installation, and local community data and resources to be leveraged to meet the service-member population's needs, which will inform whether primary data collection methods or additional secondary data are needed. The information collected and assessed through the BSH SAT informs the command about topics and resources needed to address concerns.
Behavioral Health Pulse (BH Pulse)	"BH Pulse is a survey tool that Behavioral Health Officers use to provide commanders with an assessment of behavioral health stressors across their formations, helping commanders to better understand risk factors in their units and to develop a plan for intervention. . . . 'The BH Pulse is a 15–20-minute survey that is anonymous. . . . It's offered through web/mobile or paper/pencil and is retained at brigade level and distributed at company level and requires a participation rate of 70% of the company in order to process the individual surveys.' 'BH Pulse facilitates the analysis of behavioral health (suicidality, depression, anxiety, PTSD), work environment, social relationships, deployments, sexual harassment and sexual assault, interpersonal violence, and other behaviors such as sleep, alcohol use, and unsafe driving'" (Curtis, 2022).
CAL's Annual Study of Army Leadership (CASAL)	"CAL's Annual Study of Army Leadership (CASAL) is a recurring annual CAC [Combined Arms Center] initiative, since 2005, to capture trends in leadership, leader development (LD), the operating environment and special topics. The longitudinal nature and Army-wide administration of CASAL produces valid and reliable insights that are generalizable and actionable. The findings inform senior leaders and key stakeholders about the quality and effectiveness of Army leadership, LD and impacts of the operating environment" (CAL, 2023b).
Career-Long Assessments: Athena	"Athena is an Army leader development program designed to inform and motivate Soldiers to embrace personal and professional development. Adding to the Army's culture of assessments, Athena uses batteries of assessments to increase a Soldiers self-awareness of leadership skills and behaviors, cognitive abilities, and personal traits and attributes. Assessment batteries are strategically selected to [align with] the leadership skills being developed at a number of Army schools. For each assessment completed, students receive a feedback report with their scores and information about how to interpret their scores" (CAL, 2023a).

Army Data Source Name	Summary
Command Assessment Program Peer and Subordinate Assessments (Lieutenant Colonel Army Commander Evaluation Tool, Colonel Army Commander Evaluation Tool, Army Leader Assessment Tool, and Enlisted Leader Assessment Tool)	The Command Assessment Program is an ongoing program in which people get 360-degree feedback from peers and subordinates about their leadership effectiveness related to the Army's leadership requirements model, which was defined by Army Doctrine Publication 6-22 (2019). The assessment provides an opportunity for peers and subordinates to assess the person based on past observable leadership behaviors. These instruments also provide a more complete understanding of the person's capabilities relative to the demands of command and key positions from those who have unique insights into the person's leadership effectiveness. (For more information, see U.S. Army, 2022.)
Commander's Risk Reduction Toolkit (CRRT)	The CRRT is a web-based system that helps command teams from the company through the Army level assess individual and unit risk by addressing 25 risk factors across such areas as suicidality, drug and alcohol misuse, safety, criminality, and administrative actions. Battalion and Company Command teams (commanders, command sergeants major, and first sergeants) are the only personnel who can see both individuals' and units' risk. Brigade and above Commander teams and their designated representatives can see only aggregated unit-level risk to see patterns and trends of risk to best apply resources. The risk picture provided by the CRRT is designed to work in conjunction with the readiness picture provided by the Army Vantage Readiness Tracker, which is located within the same system and is designed to provide a more comprehensive picture of the true readiness of the formations.
Community Strengths and Themes Assessment (CSTA)	CSTA "assists commands in the development of a responsive and holistic community support plan" (Defense Centers for Public Heath, undated). The CSTA survey is an online questionnaire for service members, dependents, civilians, retirees, and anyone associated with the military community. There are seven sections: (1) physical health, (2) behavioral and emotional health, (3) social and environmental health, (4) spiritual health, (5) family health, (6) programs and services, and (7) demographics.
Drug and Alcohol Management Information System (DAMIS)	"DAMIS is a management tool which supports . . . the treatment, counseling, and rehabilitation of individuals who participate in the Army Substance Abuse Program. It identifies trends, judges the magnitude of drug and alcohol abuse, and measures the effectiveness of drug and alcohol prevention efforts in the Army. PII [personal identifiable information] collect[ed] includes personal, medical, and military information" (U.S. Army, 2020).
Equal Employment Opportunity (EEO) iComplaints	iComplaints tracks EEO complaint cases. "It is the policy of the [Department of the Army] to provide EEO in Federal employment, consistent with Federal merit system principles and applicable law, for all persons, to prohibit discrimination in employment because of race, color, religion, sex, national origin, reprisal, disability, age, sexual orientation, gender identity, status as a parent, or other impermissible basis, and to promote the full realization of EEO through a continuing diversity and inclusion program" (Army Regulation 690-12, 2019).

Army Data Source Name	Summary
Family Advocacy System of Records (FASOR)	"Army FASOR is a web-based application which operates on the Xtendable platform which supports data input, incident determination processes, case management, and program management for the Army Family Advocacy Program. Historically, it has supported 20,000 to 25,000 new incidents per fiscal year" (GovTribe, 2014). FASOR is the database that houses the Army central registry (i.e., the registry is within FASOR) of only active-duty personnel.
Integrated Case Reporting System (ICRS)	ICRS is an Army web-based application that captures and records all data for reported incidents of sexual harassment and allows users to run annual reports based on the DoD sexual harassment template for their units, installations, or commands based on their user roles or access. Data for individual cases excluding PII are also available. Data in ICRS are populated by sexual assault response coordinators from sexual harassment complaints (including anonymous, formal, and informal).
Joint Analytical Real-time Virtual Information Sharing System (JARVISS)	JARVISS is "Army software designed to target criminal activity and provide natural disaster info in and around Army installations and stand-alone facilities" (DoD, undated). JARVISS is available as an application for Apple and Android, in which users can view incidents in real time in their areas. Users must be DoD-affiliated to access JARVISS.
Medical Readiness Assessment Tool (MRAT)	"The Medical Readiness Assessment Tool (MRAT) is a cloud-based, three-applications-in-one electronic decision support and screening tool that allows U.S. Army clinicians and non-clinician leaders to more proactively maintain Soldier readiness. The primary objective of the MRAT is to provide timely holistic assessments and interventions to preserve unit readiness to at-risk Soldiers. Within the constraints of Health Insurance Portability and Accountability Act and privacy rules, the MRAT provides leaders and clinicians a powerful tool for mitigating factors that threaten individual medical readiness" (Frady, 2015).
	The tool displays the composite risk and component risk factors for *permanent medical nondeployable status*, which is defined as a permanent level 3 or 4 profile in the physical (P), upper extremities (U), lower extremities (L), or psychiatric / stability (S) domains of the "PULHES" system.
	The tool identifies relative risk of nondeployment six months into the future for every active-duty soldier every month. The MRAT dashboard displays associated readiness risk, including factors such as opiate prescriptions, health care utilization, and time on profile. Clinicians can use this information to identify high-risk soldiers.
Military Equal Opportunity (MEO) database	MEO is "the right of all Service members to serve, advance, and be evaluated based on only individual merit, fitness, capability, and performance in an environment free of prohibited discrimination on the basis of race, color, national origin, religion, sex, gender identity, or sexual orientation" (DoDI 1350.02, 2022, p. 37). In the MEO database, the Army uses spreadsheets to track and report "alleged incidents of hazing in three database management systems as part of its Equal Opportunity (EO) offices, the Inspector General (IG), and the Criminal Investigation Command" (DoD, 2022, p. 8). The MEO database will be integrated with SHARP's ICRS to collect and track data complaints.
Military Justice Online (MJO)	The Army manages and tracks courts-martial and other military justice actions through its MJO application.

Army Data Source Name	Summary
Person-Event Data Environment (PDE)	The PDE is sponsored by the AAG and managed by its Research Facilitation Lab. The PDE's purpose is to provide an environment for research and analysis and for the development and potential hosting of analytics applications and reports. The PDE provides an integrated solution to significantly enhance access to manpower, personnel, medical, and other relevant data. The vision is to provide a self-service and collaborative environment that allows those who need such data to retrieve and analyze the data with a minimum amount of assistance and to give DoD and Army senior leaders timely and actionable information. The PDE includes a project governance suite that allows users to define a project, invite team members to join the project (subject to vetting and authorization), specify datasets from a data catalog, conduct the analyses or development, and publish or deploy the results with controlled or open availability. The PDE portal encourages data and idea sharing and moves analysis and development processes closer to a collaborative and self-service model that produces best results. The PDE provides a central data store with Extract Transform Load (ETL) services, an analysis enclave without PII or protected health information, and a production reporting environment. Additionally, PDE applications may be hosted within AAG-supported environments (e.g., on premises data center, the cArmy Cloud). Data in the PDE central data store are maintained, transformed, and used in accordance with all applicable laws, regulations, and DoD and Department of the Army policies for the protection of human subjects and for the security of individually identifiable data. All users and teams conducting projects in the PDE or using data in the PDE must agree that such information will be secured as required by law, regulation, and Army policy. The PDE supports component development for visualization, analytics processing, and capture of data. These efforts (referred to as *PDE Reports* and *PDE Applications*) must follow standard AAG software development practices, which conform to DoD and Army business, technical, and security requirements. Finally, the PDE promotes a shared services model to leverage the core financial investment into the PDE's processes, tools, and capacity. Projects requiring technical capabilities or capacities beyond the core offering will need to provide above baseline resourcing. Additionally, new tools requested in the PDE will be assessed, approved, and deployed consistent with the DoD Risk Management Framework.
Strategic Management System (SMS) Army Suicide Prevention Program (ASPP)	The SMS ASPP provides installation program managers, as well as Army command program managers, with the ability to look at a breakdown of deaths in their area of operations, based on duty location and death location. Two common operating pictures break down cases based on demographic and characteristic data.
SMS drug testing	Drug testing professionals use the SMS to visualize and quickly assess drug testing efforts in their footprint. Eight common operating pictures are provided to all professionals, and they can use SMS filters and permissions to provide their footprint data to users.
SMS Sexual Harassment/Assault Response and Prevention (SHARP)	The SMS SHARP dashboard is a visualization tool that ingests data from DSAID and ICRS to assist SHARP professionals in creating products to inform their leadership. It is part of the SMS, which was developed by Spider Strategies for the SHARP Program. According to Spider Strategies (undated), "There are currently more than 400 SHARP metrics and nearly a dozen SHARP common operating pictures and custom reports available through the SHARP-SMS deployment of Spider Impact." SMS SHARP is developed in coordination with the I-PAG.

Army Data Source Name	Summary
Unit Risk Inventory (URI) and Re-integration Unit Risk Inventory (R-URI) Surveys	"The Unit Risk Inventory Survey, or URI, is an opportunity for Soldiers to give an honest, anonymous assessment of their well being, and offers commanders the ability to gauge unit readiness and resilience. The URI is an anonymous questionnaire designed to screen for high-risk behaviors and attitudes that affect unit readiness and personal resiliency. The survey is an assessment tool that assists commanders in determining the occurrences of high-risk behavior through self-reported information" (Davenport, 2019).
	The R-URI is an alternative version of the URI that is administered to units after deployment. The R-URI contains many of the same questions as the original URI and adds questions related to soldiers' experiences since returning to their home station. "The R-URI applies an audit score to identify drinking problems, provides commanders with insight on unit high-risk behavior, and measures high-risk behavior that has occurred during deployment and since returning" (Davenport, 2019).

Table D.2. High-Level Summary of Department of Defense Data Sources

DoD Data Source Name	Summary
Active-Duty Spouse Survey	The Active-Duty Spouse Survey is sent to military spouses, sponsored by the Office of Military Community and Family Policy, and conducted by the Defense Personnel Analytics Center's OPA every other year. A similar survey exists for reserve-component spouses and is called the *Reserve Component Spouse Survey*.
Advana	Advana is the "common enterprise data repository for the Department of Defense (DoD), required by the National Defense Authorization Act (NDAA) for Fiscal Year (FY) 2018" (Department of Defense Financial Management Regulation 7000.14-R, 2023). It is intended to provide an advanced analytic platform for data sources across DoD, including DoD data sources that contain information on the occurrence of and risk and protective factors for the harmful behaviors focused on in this report (e.g., DEOCS, WGRA, DSAID). Data continue to be integrated into Advana.
Armed Forces Medical Examiner System (AFMES)	AFMES is the medical examiner system that contains information on deaths, causes of death, and toxicology reports. "As the only medicolegal death investigation system of the U.S. federal government, AFMES is the only medical examiner system authorized to support the DoD and other federal agencies with comprehensive forensic investigative services, to include forensic pathology, DNA forensics, forensic toxicology and medical mortality surveillance" (DHA, 2022).
Behavioral Health Data Portal (BHDP)	BHDP is a real-time web-based system used by behavioral health staff to collect, track, and display patients' current and past assessment data, behavioral health diagnoses, and treatment plans. BHDP is used by patients receiving outpatient care for behavioral health, mental health, or substance use issues. The provider documents the patient's diagnosis and treatment plan, in addition to rating the patient's risk of harm to self and to others and risk of being harmed by others. Various screening measures are completed by the patient. The system also produces a clinical note for practitioners related to each visit. The information can be accessed through a dashboard that reflects the scores on various screening measures completed by the patient; a research database with raw data is also available, pending DHA approval.

DoD Data Source Name	Summary
Defense Casualty Information Processing System (DCIPS)	DCIPS "provides the four military service casualty and mortuary affairs offices with a single and standard automated support capability. The system allows for on-line receipt of casualty messages; provides cross-functional case management of casualties to include, casualty incident, disposition of remains, mortuary affairs, prior conflicts and wars, personal effects, remains tracking and permits interactive update and data exchange with casualty assistance centers, mortuaries, Service casualty offices, Defense Manpower Data Center (DMDC), other DoD components; and formulates the required documents and reports" (Department of the Army, 2009).
DHA Medical Operational Data System (MODS) Electronic Profiling System (e-Profile)	The DHA MODS e-Profile "is a software application within the Medical Operational Data System (MODS) suite that allows global tracking of army Soldiers who have a temporary or permanent medical condition that may render them medically not ready to deploy" (Womack Army Medical Center, undated). Components include Medical Retention Board, Medical Evaluation Board, Physical Evaluation Board, Medical Specialty Referral for Soldiers, and other items.
Defense Medical Epidemiology Database (DMED)	"DMED provides remote access to a subset of data contained within the Defense Medical Surveillance System. DMSS contains up-to-date and historical data on diseases and medical events (e.g., hospitalizations, ambulatory visits, reportable diseases, etc.) and longitudinal data relevant to personnel characteristics and deployments experience for all active and reserve component service members. The DMED application provides a user-friendly interface to perform queries regarding disease and injury rates and relative burdens of disease in active component populations. The purpose of DMED is to standardize the epidemiologic methodology used to collect, integrate and analyze active component service member personnel and medical event data, and to provide authorized users with remote access to the summarized data. Using client-server technologies and database optimization, DMED users have unprecedented access to epidemiologic data on active component service members and tailored queries that respond in a timely and efficient manner" (DHA, 2024b).
Defense Medical Surveillance System (DMSS)	"DMSS is a longitudinal, relational database of medical events (hospitalizations, outpatient visits, reportable medical events, immunizations and deaths), personal characteristics (rank, military occupation, demographic factors), and military deployments of all Army, Navy, Air Force, Marine and Coast Guard service members over their entire military careers. These data are captured for active components, and for reserve and guard members when utilizing the Military Health System (MHS)—or civilian health care if purchased through the MHS. DMSS also captures care provided to dependent and military retirees when utilizing the MHS or civilian healthcare if purchased through the MHS" (DHA, 2023c).
Defense Organizational Climate Survey (DEOCS)	"The Defense Organizational Climate Survey (DEOCS) is a unit-level climate survey that all military commanders and Department of Defense (DoD) civilian organization leaders are required to administer to their unit or organization within 120 days of a change in command, and annually thereafter." (DoD OPA, p. 1).
DEOCS Commanders Dashboard	"The Interactive Dashboard is a part of the *DEOCS* Portal and is the main way that users can check response rates, as well as view or download the results of their *DEOCS* after the survey has ended" (DoD, 2023, p.1). The objectives of the climate dashboard, which are outlined in the Plan of Action and Milestones, are to (1) display unit-level climate metrics, including full DEOCS results, and (2) connect commanders with resources to address identified climate issues.

DoD Data Source Name	Summary
Defense Sexual Assault Incident Database (DSAID)	"DSAID is a centralized case-level database, which collects and maintains information on sexual assaults involving Armed Forces members," including tracking and reporting on sexual assault-related retaliation data (Sexual Harassment/Assault Prevention Program, undated).
Department of Defense Suicide Event Report (DoDSER)	"The Department of Defense Suicide Event Report system standardizes suicide surveillance across the Army, Marine Corps, Navy, Air Force, and Space Force to support the Department of Defense's suicide prevention mission. The DoDSER tracks a variety of suicide-related risk factors and other contextual factors for suicide events that occur among U.S. service men and women. All identified suicide deaths and attempts as well as some other suicide-related behaviors (such as intentional self-harm and suicidal ideation) require DoDSER form submissions" (DHA, 2023a).
Family Advocacy Program (FAP) Central Registry	The DoD FAP Central Registry consists of data submitted from each military service. "For more than 40 years, the Office of the Secretary of Defense (OSD) Family Advocacy Program (FAP) has worked to prevent and respond to child abuse and neglect and domestic abuse in military families . . . [and] provides the child abuse and neglect and domestic abuse incident data from the FAP Central Registry for Fiscal Year (FY) 2021, as required by Section 574 of the National Defense Authorization Act (NDAA) . . ." (DoD, 2022c, p. 8)

Each service has its own FAP and data collection. "The U.S. Army Family Advocacy Program (FAP) is dedicated to domestic and Child abuse prevention, education, prompt reporting, investigation, intervention and treatment. The Army provides a variety of services to Soldiers and Families to enhance their relationship skills and improve their quality of life. This mission is accomplished through a variety of groups, seminars, workshops and counseling and intervention services" (U.S. Army, undated-c). |
| Health Related Behaviors Survey (HRBS) | The HRBS is DoD's flagship survey for self-reported data on the health and well-being of service members. Since 1980, the survey has assessed health-related behaviors that may impact readiness. Topics include health promotion and disease prevention, substance use (including alcohol, tobacco, and illicit drugs), behavioral health, physical health and functional limitations, and sexual behavior and health. Over time, the survey has included various special topics of interest to DoD. Data from the survey are also used to compare the military population to the U.S. civilian population as well as to U.S. Department of Health and Human Services' Healthy People objectives (DHA, 2024a).

Since 2015, RAND has been responsible for the HRBS; the information presented in this report reflects the RAND version of the survey. |
| Law Enforcement Defense Data Exchange (LE D-DEx) | LE D-DEx is the authorized DoD integrated criminal justice information sharing system. LE D-DEx allows "local and state agencies to share their law enforcement records with each other to assist with investigations and crime analysis across jurisdictional lines" (Naval Criminal Investigative Services, undated) |

DoD Data Source Name	Summary
Military and Family Life Counseling (MFLC) data	MFLC data are part of the Military OneSource Data Warehouse. "Data Warehouse is a powerful online application that lets the Office of the Secretary of Defense, headquarter points of contact and installation decision makers easily find and analyze data about non-medical counseling activities among service members and their families" (Military OneSource, undated).
	"The MFLC Activity Report summarizes the non-medical MFLC Program services provided to military personnel and their family members. The MFLC Activity Report, along with monthly Military OneSource reports and Duty-to-Warn and Mandated Reporting reports, may be accessed by installation points of contact via the Data Warehouse" (DoD, 2022b, p. 13).
Military Health System Data Repository (MDR)	"The Military Health System Data Repository (MDR) is the centralized data repository that captures, validates, integrates, distributes, and archives Defense Health Agency (DHA) corporate health care data" (DHA, 2019b).
Military Health System Management Analysis and Reporting Tool (MHS MART or M2)	"The Military Health System Management Analysis and Reporting Tool (MHS MART), most commonly called M2, is a MDR-derived data mart using web-based cube technology designed for easy self-service to enterprise data. M2 is a powerful ad-hoc query tool used to manage and oversee operations worldwide" (DHA, 2019a).
On-Site Installation Evaluation (OSIE) DEOCS	The OSIE DEOCS tool incorporates DEOCS data since January 2021 to visualize 11 risk factors and 11 protective factors at the unit level, installation level, and various levels of command. The tool is accessed via Advana.

DoD Data Source Name	Summary
OSIE Resilience Index	The OSIE Resilience Index is a tool accessed via Advana that incorporates multiple data sources as part of five domains according to an SEM, a public health framework that enables scholars to better understand the causal processes behind incidents of harm or violence, including why and how individuals are at risk or protected from harm or violence. The tool produces a composite score for the resilience level at the installation level. The five domains included in the resilience index used to assess a site's overall protection for harmful behaviors are: 1. community resilience 2. installation resilience 3. leadership resilience 4. workplace resilience 5. individual resilience. Data sources for each domain include the following: • Community resilience risk (2022–2023): County health rankings of the county surrounding the site provide an indicator of the risk of the community in which service members, civilians, and families live; these measures were developed by the University of Wisconsin. • Installation resilience risk (2018–2022): Incidents of death by suicide, substantiated incidents of domestic abuse and child abuse, estimated prevalence of sexual assault and sexual harassment, and reporting of sexual assault provide indicators of the site's historical risk for harmful behaviors; this domain includes data from WGRA, DSAID, FAP, and the Defense Suicide Prevention Office. • Leadership resilience risk (2021–2022): Assessments of commander, noncommissioned officer, and immediate supervisor's leadership (i.e., passive, toxic, transformational) provide an indicator of the leadership's contribution to an unhealthy climate; this domain includes DEOCS data. • Workplace resilience risk (2018; 2021–2022): Assessments of such factors as stress, morale, fairness, inclusion, cohesion, engagement, commitment, and trust in the military system provide an indicator of the workplace climate; this domain includes data from DEOCS and WGRA. • Individual resilience risk (2021–2022): Assessments of individuals' experiences of sexism, sexually harassing behaviors, racially harassing behaviors, alcohol use, and sense of connectedness provide an indicator of personal risk; this domain includes DEOCS data.

DoD Data Source Name	Summary
Periodic Health Assessment (PHA)	"The Periodic Health Assessment is a screening tool used by the armed forces to evaluate the individual medical readiness of their service members. It can be conducted alone or can be combined with other individual medical readiness needs (e.g., dental exam and immunizations). Completed annually, the PHA consists of the following components for the service member: • A self-reported health status • Measurement and documentation of vitals (height, weight, blood pressure) • Vision screening • Review of current medical conditions with health care provider • Focused exam of identified conditions (as required) • Cardiovascular Screening Program Services (as required) • Recommendations for improvement of identified health conditions • Behavioral health screen • Laboratory services (as required) • Immunizations (as required)" (DHA, 2023b).
Post-Deployment Health Assessment (PDHA) and Post-Deployment Health Re-Assessment (PDHRA)	The PDHA and PDHRA contain data on suicide risk factors, alcohol use, and depressive symptoms postdeployment or postredeployment, respectively.
QuickCompass of Sexual Assault Responders (QSAR)	The QSAR provides information to DoD on sexual assault responders' training, their access to and relationships with command and other professionals, their perceptions of resources provided to victims, the support that they receive in their profession, and their personal wellbeing.
Service Academy Gender Relations (SAGR) survey	"The purpose of the 2022 Service Academy Gender Relations Survey (2022 SAGR) is to provide the official prevalence estimates for unwanted sexual contact and MEO violations among students in the service academies in the past academic program year and statistical change of those estimates over time. The 2022 SAGR also assesses sexual assault/sexual harassment reporting and complaint processes; measures cadet/midshipman attitudes toward and perceptions of sexual assault and sexual harassment programs and policies designed to reduce the occurrence of these unwanted behaviors; and examines the gender relations climate(s)" (DoD OPA, 2023).
Status of Forces Survey (SOFS)	SOFS is an annual DoD web-based survey of active-duty and reserve members that is designed to "assess retention, satisfaction, tempo, stress, and readiness" (DoD OPA, undated-b).
Study to Assess Risk and Resilience in Service Members - Longitudinal Study (STARRS-LS)	STARRS-LS is a continuation of the Army STARRS project, which started in 2009 in response to the rising suicide rate in the Army. Being epidemiological and neurobiological, the study was designed to characterize the risk factors and protective factors associated with self-harm and related mental or behavioral health problems. Army STARRS consisted of eight separate component studies, and STARRS-LS collects longitudinal data from a prospective cohort derived from 72,000

DoD Data Source Name	Summary
	soldiers who enrolled during Army STARRS and consented to allow the linkage of their Army STARRS survey data to their Army and DoD administrative data.

The studies conducted under Army STARRS are the following:

- The Historical Administrative Data Study (HADS) was an analysis of 2004–2009 administrative data from Army and DoD from 37 sources that were obtained and integrated by the research team. The HADS dataset has expanded to include all soldiers (regular, guard, and reserve) who ever served since January 1, 2004 (or more than 3 million people) with more than 50 contributing data sources. The HADS dataset currently spans 2004 to 2019 and is updated at least semiannually. No public-use dataset is available, but the data are available to approved researchers and analysts via the AAG or directly from the source data systems.

- The New Soldier Study comprised questionnaires and neurocognitive tests administered to new trainees at Ft. Jackson, Ft. Benning, and Ft. Leonard Wood between September 2011 and November 2012.

- The All Army Study comprised questionnaires administered to established soldiers (i.e., not in initial training status) at more than 50 Army sites worldwide between January 2011 and April 2013.

- The Soldier Health Outcomes Study A was a case-control study conducted between November 2011 and December 2013 to identify differences between soldiers from the All Army Study and soldiers who were hospitalized for a suicide attempt; this study included questionnaires and neurocognitive tests. No public use dataset is available.

- The Soldier Health Outcomes Study B was a psychological autopsy case-control study of 150 soldiers who died by suicide between March 2012 and January 2014; interviews were conducted with next of kin and first-line supervisors. No public-use dataset is available.

- The Pre/Post Deployment Study was a longitudinal study designed to assess effects of deployment on soldiers over time; four surveys were conducted, including a predeployment baseline and three postdeployment timepoints (two to three weeks, three months, and nine months), between January 2012 and April 2014.

- The Criminal Investigation Division Study was a study of Army Criminal Investigation Division file reports for 1,311 deaths of Army service members between 2005 and 2009 as a result of suicide, accidents, traffic fatalities, justifiable homicides, or undetermined causes. No public use dataset is available.

- The Clinical Reappraisal Study was a validation study of mental disorder diagnostic screening tools used in STARRS questionnaires from March 2012 to November 2012. No public use dataset is available.

STARRS-LS questionnaires (Waves 1–4 with a total of approximately 14,500 participants, who are a mix of serving soldiers and veterans) are similar to the questionnaires administered in the All Army Study, New Soldier Study, and the Pre/Post-Deployment Study. They include modules on employment, education, substance use (tobacco, alcohol, and drugs), depression, high mood (i.e., manic episodes), anxiety, anger attacks, panic, self-harm (including suicide attempts, ideation, and self-harming behaviors without intention to commit suicide), stressful experiences, firearm ownership, deployment experiences, personal relationships, family income, and childhood experiences.

DoD Data Source Name	Summary
	Wave 1 (2016–2017), Wave 2 (2018–2019), and Wave 3 (2020–2022) of STARRS-LS questionnaires have completed data collection. Data from Waves 1 and 2 are already available as public use files through ICPSR at the University of Michigan. Wave 3 data became available in ICPSR in Fall 2023. Wave 4 data collection is underway, will finish in April 2024, and be available in ICPSR later that year.
Workplace and Equal Opportunity (WEO) survey	This DoD survey of active-duty and reserve members was "designed to assess self-reported experiences of and the climate surrounding racial/ethnic harassment and discrimination in the military" (DoD OPA, undated-a).
Workplace and Gender Relations Survey of Military Members: Active Component (WGRA)	This DoD survey of military members "provides the DoD's official estimates of the prevalence of gender discrimination, sexual harassment, and unwanted sexual contact in the Military" (DoD OPA, undated-c).

Table D.3. High-Level Summary of Army Personnel Databases

Army Personnel Database Name	Summary
Total Army Personnel Database (TAPDB)	This database provides a person-level monthly snapshot of Army active officer (TAPDB-AO), active enlisted (TAPDB-AE), reserve (TAPDB-R), and National Guard (TAPDB-NG) service members. The files include demographics (e.g., sex, age, marital status) and career attributes (e.g., pay grade, military occupational specialty [MOS]). TAPDB is maintained by the U.S. Army Human Resources Command.
Defense Enrollment Eligibility Reporting System Point in Time Extract (DEERS PITE)	This database provides a person-level monthly point-in-time snapshot of all DoD beneficiaries, including sponsors (e.g., active duty, reserves, national guard, retired) and their dependents (e.g., spouse, children). The files include demographics (e.g., sex, age, marital status) and career attributes (e.g., pay grade, MOS). DEERS PITE data can be requested directly through DMDC or accessed through the MDR and M2 platforms. DEERS PITE is maintained by the DMDC.
Active-Duty Military Personnel Master and Transaction File (ADMF/ADT)	This database provides person-level monthly information for all active-duty uniformed personnel across all military branches of service. The files include demographics (e.g., sex, age, marital status) and career attributes (e.g., pay grade, MOS). ADMF/ADT is maintained by the DMDC.

Abbreviations

AAG	Army Analytics Group
AFMES	Armed Forces Medical Examiner System
ALERTS	Army Law Enforcement Reporting and Tracking System
ARAP	Army Readiness Assessment Program
ASAP	Army Substance Abuse Program
ASMIS 2.0	Army Safety Management Information System
ASPP	Army Suicide Prevention Program
BHDP	Behavioral Health Data Portal
BH Pulse	Behavioral Health Pulse
BSH SAT	Behavioral and Social Health Self-Assessment Tool
BSHOP RFI	Behavioral and Social Health Outcomes Practice Request for Information
CAL	Center for Army Leadership
CASAL	CAL's Annual Study of Army Leadership
CRRT	Commander's Risk Reduction Toolkit
CSTA	Community Strengths and Themes Assessment
DAMIS	Drug and Alcohol Management Information System
DCIPS	Defense Casualty Information Processing System
DEERS PITE	Defense Enrollment Eligibility Reporting System Point in Time Extract
DEOCS	Defense Organizational Climate Survey
DHA	Defense Health Agency
DMDC	Defense Manpower Data Center
DMED	Defense Medical Epidemiology Database
DMSS	Defense Medical Surveillance System
DoD	U.S. Department of Defense
DoDI	Department of Defense Instruction
DoDSER	Department of Defense Suicide Event Report
DSAID	Defense Sexual Assault Incident Database
EEO	equal employment opportunity
e-Profile	Electronic Profiling System
FAP	Family Advocacy Program
FASOR	Family Advocacy System of Records
GAO	U.S. Government Accountability Office
HADS	Historical Administrative Data Study
HRBS	Health Related Behaviors Survey

ICPSR	Inter-university Consortium for Political and Social Research
ICRS	Integrated Case Reporting System
I-PAG	Integrated Prevention Advisory Group
IPD	Integrated Prevention Division
JARVISS	Joint Analytical Real-time Virtual Information Sharing System
LE D-DEx	Law Enforcement Defense Data Exchange
M2	Military Health System Management Analysis and Reporting Tool
MDR	Military Health System Data Repository
MEO	Military Equal Opportunity
MFLC	Military and Family Life Counseling
MHS	Military Health System
MHS MART	Military Health System Management Analysis and Reporting Tool
MJO	Military Justice Online
MODS	Medical Operational Data System
MOS	military occupational specialty
MRAT	Medical Readiness Assessment Tool
OPA	Office of People Analytics
OSIE	on-site installation evaluation
PDE	Person-Event Data Environment
PDHA	Post-Deployment Health Assessment
PDHRA	Post-Deployment Health Re-Assessment
PHA	Periodic Health Assessment
PII	personal identifiable information
PPoA 2.0	Prevention Plan of Action 2.0
QSAR	QuickCompass of Sexual Assault Responders
R-URI	Re-Integration Unit Risk Inventory
SAGR	Service Academy Gender Relations survey
SEM	social-ecological model
SHARP	Sexual Harassment/Assault Response and Prevention
SME	subject-matter expert
SMS	Strategic Management System
SOFS	Status of Forces Survey
STARRS	Study to Assess Risk and Resilience in Service Members
STARRS-LS	Study to Assess Risk and Resilience in Service Members – Longitudinal Study
URI	Unit Risk Inventory
WEO	Workplace and Equal Opportunity
WGRA	Workplace and Gender Relations Survey of Military Members: Active Component

Bibliography

Acosta, Joie D., Matthew Chinman, and Amy L. Shearer, *Countering Sexual Assault and Sexual Harassment in the U.S. Military: Lessons from RAND Research*, RAND Corporation, RR-A1318-1, 2021. As of August 3, 2023:
https://www.rand.org/pubs/research_reports/RRA1318-1.html

Army Doctrine Publication 6-22, *Army Leadership and the Profession*, Department of the Army, July 2019.

Army Regulation 190-45, *Law Enforcement Reporting*, Department of the Army, September 27, 2016.

Army Regulation 600-85, *The Army Substance Abuse Program*, Department of the Army, July 23, 2020.

Army Regulation 690-12, *Equal Employment Opportunity and Diversity*, Department of the Army, December 12, 2019.

CAL—*See* Center for Army Leadership.

Calkins, Avery, Matthew Cefalu, Terry L. Schell, Linda Cottrell, Sarah O. Meadows, and Rebecca L. Collins, *Sexual Assault Experiences in the Active-Component Army: Variation by Year, Gender, Sexual Orientation, and Installation Risk Level*, RAND Corporation, RR-A1385-2, 2022. As of August 3, 2023:
https://www.rand.org/pubs/research_reports/RRA1385-2.html

Center for Army Leadership, "Athena," webpage, 2023a. As of April 4, 2024:
https://cal.army.mil/Athena/

Center for Army Leadership, "CAL's Annual Study of Army Leadership (CASAL)," webpage, 2023b. As of April 4, 2024:
https://cal.army.mil/Resource-Library/CASAL/

Chinman, Matthew, Patricia A. Ebener, Coreen Farris, Amy L. Shearer, and Joie D. Acosta, *Getting To Outcomes®: Guide for Strengthening Sexual Assault Prevention Activities in the Military*, RAND Corporation, TL-A746-1, 2021. As of August 3, 2023:
https://www.rand.org/pubs/tools/TLA746-1.html

Curtis, Chet, "Army Introduces Behavioral Health Pulse Tool to Help Leaders," U.S. Army, January 14, 2022.

Davenport, Kyra, "Unit Risk Inventory Survey Helps Gauge Readiness, Resilience," U.S. Army, September 24, 2019.

Defense Centers for Public Heath, "Community Strengths and Themes Assessment (CSTA)," webpage, undated. As of July 1, 2024:
https://phpubapps.health.mil/Survey/se/2511374548575240

Defense Health Agency, "M2," fact sheet, March 2019a.

Defense Health Agency, "MDR," fact sheet, March 2019b.

Defense Health Agency, "Armed Forces Medical Examiner System," fact sheet, May 2022.

Defense Health Agency, "Department of Defense Suicide Event Report," webpage, last updated July 11, 2023a. As of April 5, 2024:
https://health.mil/Military-Health-Topics/Centers-of-Excellence/Psychological-Health-Center-of-Excellence/Department-of-Defense-Suicide-Event-Report

Defense Health Agency, "Periodic Health Assessment," webpage, last updated July 11, 2023b. As of April 5, 2024:
https://www.health.mil/Military-Health-Topics/Health-Readiness/Reserve-Health-Readiness-Program/Our-Services/PHA

Defense Health Agency, "Frequently Asked Questions," webpage, last updated September 22, 2023c. As of April 5, 2024:
https://www.health.mil/Military-Health-Topics/Health-Readiness/AFHSD/Frequently-Asked-Questions

Defense Health Agency, "Survey of Health-Related Behaviors," webpage, last updated February 8, 2024a. As of April 5, 2024:
https://www.health.mil/Military-Health-Topics/Access-Cost-Quality-and-Safety/Health-Care-Program-Evaluation/Survey-of-Health-Related-Behaviors

Defense Health Agency, "Defense Medical Epidemiology Database," webpage, last updated March 25, 2024b. As of April 5, 2024:
https://www.health.mil/Military-Health-Topics/Health-Readiness/AFHSD/Functional-Information-Technology-Support/Defense-Medical-Epidemiology-Database

Defense Logistics Agency Information Operations, "DLA Expanding Use of DOD Advanced Analytics Tool," Defense Logistics Agency, June 17, 2022.

Department of Defense Financial Management Regulation 7000.14-R, *Advana – Common Enterprise Data Repository for the Department of Defense*, Vol. 1, Chapter 10, June 2023.

Department of Defense Instruction 1010.04, *Problematic Substance Use by DoD Personnel*, incorporating change 1, Office of the Under Secretary of Defense for Personnel and Readiness, May 6, 2020.

Department of Defense Instruction 1010.16, *Technical Procedures for the Military Drug Abuse Testing Program*, Office of the Under Secretary of Defense for Personnel and Readiness, June 15, 2020.

Department of Defense Instruction 1020.03, *Harassment Prevention and Response in the Armed Forces*, incorporating change 2, Office of the Under Secretary of Defense for Personnel and Readiness, December 20, 2022.

Department of Defense Instruction 1350.02, *DoD Military Equal Opportunity Program*, incorporating change 1, Office of the Under Secretary of Defense for Personnel and Readiness, December 20, 2022.

Department of Defense Instruction 3216.02, *Protection of Human Subjects and Adherence to Ethical Standards in DoD-Conducted and -Supported Research*, incorporating change 1, U.S. Department of Defense, June 29, 2022.

Department of Defense Instruction 6400.06, *DoD Coordinated Community Response to Domestic Abuse Involving DoD Military and Certain Affiliated Personnel*, incorporating change 2, Office of the Under Secretary of Defense for Personnel and Readiness, May 16, 2023.

Department of Defense Instruction 6400.09, *DoD Policy on Integrated Primary Prevention of Self-Directed Harm and Prohibited Abuse or Harm*, Office of the Under Secretary of Defense for Personnel and Readiness, September 11, 2020.

Department of Defense Instruction 6490.16, *Defense Suicide Prevention Program*, Office of the Under Secretary of Defense for Personnel and Readiness, incorporating change 3, February 2, 2023.

Department of Defense Instruction 6495.02, Volume 1, *Sexual Assault Prevention and Response: Program Procedures*, incorporating change 7, September 6, 2022.

Department of the Army, "Defense Casualty Information Processing System (DCIPS) AR 600-8-1 Army Casualty Program," Request for Disposition Authority, April 20, 2009.

DHA—*See* Defense Health Agency.

DoD—*See* U.S. Department of Defense.

DoDI—*See* Department of Defense Instruction.

DoD, OPA—*See* U.S. Department of Defense, Office of People Analytics.

Durant, Lauren E., Michael P. Carey, and Kerstin E. E. Schroder, "Effects of Anonymity, Gender, and Erotophilia on the Quality of Data Obtained from Self-Reports of Socially Sensitive Behaviors," *Journal of Behavioral Medicine*, Vol. 25, No. 5, November 2002.

Farris, Coreen, Terry L. Schell, Lisa H. Jaycox, and Robin L. Beckman, *Perceived Retaliation Against Military Sexual Assault Victims*, RAND Corporation, RR-2380-OSD, 2021. As of August 2, 2023:
https://www.rand.org/pubs/research_reports/RR2380.html

Fink, David S., M. Shayne Gallaway, Marijo B. Tamburrino, Israel Liberzon, Philip Chan, Gregory H. Cohen, Edwin Shirley, Toyomi Goto, Nicole D'Arcangelo, Thomas Fine, Philip L. Reed, Joseph R. Calabrese, and Sandro Galea, "Onset of Alcohol Use Disorders and Comorbid Psychiatric Disorders in a Military Cohort: Are There Critical Periods for Prevention of Alcohol Use Disorders?" *Prevention Science*, Vol. 17, No. 3, December 2015.

Frady, Kirk, "Medical Readiness Assessment Tool (MRAT)," U.S. Army, November 24, 2015.

GAO—*See* U.S. Government Accountability Office.

GovTribe, "U. S. Army Family Advocacy System of Record (FASOR)," Solicitation # W9124J-14-T-0007, Mission and Installation Contracting Command, Joint Base San Antonio–Fort Sam Houston, August 7, 2014. As of May 29, 2024:
https://govtribe.com/opportunity/federal-contract-opportunity/u-dot-s-dot-army-family-advocacy-system-of-record-fasor-w9124j14t0007

Integrated Prevention Advisory Group, "What Is the Integrated Prevention Advisory Group (I-PAG)?" webpage, undated. As of April 4, 2024:
https://www.armyresilience.army.mil/IPAG/index.html

I-PAG—*See* Integrated Prevention Advisory Group.

Kessler, Ronald C., Lisa J. Colpe, Carol S. Fullerton, Nancy Gebler, James A. Naifeh, Matthew K. Nock, Nancy A. Sampson, Michael Schoenbaum, Alan M. Zaslavsky, Murray B. Stein, Robert J. Ursano, and Steven G. Heeringa, "Design of the Army Study to Assess Risk and Resilience in Servicemembers (Army STAARS)," *International Journal of Methods in Psychiatric Research*, Vol. 22, No. 4, December 2013.

Matthews, Miriam, Andrew R. Morral, Terry L. Schell, Matthew Cefalu, Joshua Snoke, and R. J. Briggs, *Organizational Characteristics Associated with Risk of Sexual Assault and Sexual Harassment in the U.S. Army*, RAND Corporation, RR-A1013-1, 2021. As of August 3, 2023: https://www.rand.org/pubs/research_reports/RRA1013-1.html

Military OneSource, "Data Warehouse User Guide," fact sheet, undated.

Miller, Laura L., Dmitry Khodyakov, Joachim O. Hero, Lisa Wagner, Coreen Farris, Katie Feistel, Emily Dao, Julia Rollison, Rosemary Li, Jamie Ryan, Stephanie Brooks Holliday, Laurie T. Martin, and Amy L. Shearer, *Domestic Abuse in the Armed Forces: Improving Prevention and Outreach*, RAND Corporation, RR-A1550-1, 2023. As of August 3, 2023: https://www.rand.org/pubs/research_reports/RRA1550-1.html

National Defense Research Institute, *Sexual Assault and Sexual Harassment in the U.S. Military: Top-Line Estimates for Active-Duty Coast Guard Members from the 2014 RAND Military Workplace Study*, RAND Corporation, RR-944-USCG, 2014. As of August 3, 2023: https://www.rand.org/pubs/research_reports/RR944.html

Naval Criminal Investigative Service, "LInX/D-Dex," webpage, undated. As of April 17, 2024: https://www.ncis.navy.mil/Mission/Partnership-Initiatives/LInX-D-Dex/

Office of the Chief Information Officer, *Army Data Plan*, October 11, 2022.

Sadler, Anne G., Ann M. Cheney, Michelle A. Mengeling, Brenda M. Booth, James C. Torner, and Lance Brendan Young, "Servicemen's Perceptions of Male Sexual Assault and Barriers to Reporting During Active Component and Reserve/National Guard Military Service," *Journal of Interpersonal Violence*, Vol. 36, Nos. 7–8, April 2021.

Schell, Terry L., Andrew R. Morral, Matthew Cefalu, Coreen Farris, and Miriam Matthews, *Risk Factors for Sexual Assault and Sexual Harassment in the U.S. Military: Findings from the 2014 RAND Military Workplace Study*, RAND Corporation, RR-870/9-OSD, 2021. As of August 3, 2023: https://www.rand.org/pubs/research_reports/RR870z9.html

Singer, Eleanor, Dawn R. Von Thurn, and Esther R. Miller, "Confidentiality Assurances and Response: A Quantitative Review of the Experimental Literature," *Public Opinion Quarterly*, Vol. 59, No. 1, Spring 1995.

Sexual Harassment/Assault Prevention Program, "Frequently Asked Questions," webpage, undated. As of July 1, 2024: https://www.armyresilience.army.mil/sharp/pages/faq.html

Singer, Eleanor, Dawn R. Von Thurn, and Esther R. Miller, "Confidentiality Assurances and Response: A Quantitative Review of the Experimental Literature," *Public Opinion Quarterly*, Vol. 59, No. 1, Spring 1995.

Spider Strategies, "U.S. Army SHARP Tracks & Visualizes Initiative Effectiveness with Spider Impact," webpage, undated. As of April 4, 2024: https://www.spiderstrategies.com/customer/sharp/

Stone, Deborah M., Kristin M. Holland, Brad Bartholow, Joseph E. Logan, Wendy LiKamWa McIntosh, Aimee Trudeau, and Ian R. H. Rockett, "Deciphering Suicide and Other Manners of Death Associated with Drug Intoxication: A Centers for Disease Control and Prevention Consultation Meeting Summary," *American Journal of Public Health*, Vol. 107, No. 8, August 2017.

Substance Abuse and Mental Health Services Administration, *Key Substance Use and Mental Health Indicators in the United States: Results from the 2021 National Survey on Drug Use and Health*, Publication No. PEP22-07-01-005, December 2022.

Suicide Prevention and Response Independent Review Committee, *Preventing Suicide in the U.S. Military: Recommendations from the Suicide Prevention and Response Independent Committee*, U.S. Department of Defense, February 2023.

U.S. Army, "ARAP: Army Readiness Assessment Program," webpage, undated-a. As of April 4, 2024:
https://earap.safety.army.mil

U.S. Army, "ASMIS 2.0," webpage, undated-b. As of April 4, 2024:
https://safety.army.mil/MEDIA/ASMIS2

U.S. Army, "Family Advocacy Programs (FAP)," webpage, undated-c. As of April 4, 2024:
https://myarmybenefits.us.army.mil/Benefit-Library/Federal-Benefits/Family-Advocacy-Programs-(FAP)

U.S. Army, *Command Assessment Program (CAP) Preparation Guide*, Version 3.0, June 2022.

U.S. Army, "Privacy Impact Statement (PIA)," form, approved August 11, 2020.

U.S. Army Directorate of Prevention, Resilience and Readiness, *Army Integrated Prevention Advisory Group (I-PAG) Guide: Tactical*, Version 1.0, October 17, 2022.

U.S. Army Public Health Center, "What Is the ABHIDE?" information sheet, July 2016.

U.S. Army Public Health Center, "Behavioral Health Epidemiological Consultation (BH EPICON)," information sheet, 2017. As of April 4, 2024:
https://ph.health.mil/PHC%20Resource%20Library/EPICONInfoSheet_13Nov2017.pdf

U.S. Army Resilience Directorate, *Report: Sharp Rise in Prevalence of Sexual Assaults in Army for FY21*, October 2022.

U.S. Department of Defense, "JARVISS Software," webpage, undated. As of April 4, 2024:
https://www.defense.gov/Multimedia/Photos/igphoto/2002299070/

U.S. Department of Defense, "DSAID Basics," fact sheet, Department of Defense Sexual Assault Prevention and Response Office, November 2016.

U.S. Department of Defense, *Department of Defense Annual Report on Sexual Assault in the Military: Fiscal Year 2018*, Sexual Assault Prevention and Response (SAPRO) Office, April 2019.

U.S. Department of Defense, *Fiscal Year 2020 Annual Report for Hazing Prevention and Response in the Armed Forces*, December 2020.

U.S. Department of Defense, *Hard Truths and the Duty to Change: Recommendations from the Independent Review Commission on Sexual Assault in the Military*, July 2021.

U.S. Department of Defense, *Prevention Plan of Action 2.0 2022–2024*, Office of the Under Secretary of Defense for Personnel and Readiness, May 2022a.

U.S. Department of Defense, *Military and Family Life Counseling Program Guide*, September 2022b.

U.S. Department of Defense, *Report on Child Abuse and Neglect and Domestic Abuse in the Military for Fiscal Year 2021*, September 2022c.

U.S. Department of Defense, *DEOCS Portal: How to Use the Interactive Dashboard*, June 2023.

U.S. Department of Defense, Office of People Analytics, "2017 Workplace and Equal Opportunity Survey of Active Duty Members," webpage, undated-a. As of April 5, 2024: https://www.opa.mil/research-analysis/quality-of-work-life/workplace-climate%20/2017-workplace-and-equal-opportunity-survey-of-active-duty-members/

U.S. Department of Defense, Office of People Analytics, "Status of Forces Surveys," webpage, undated-b. As of April 5, 2024: https://www.opa.mil/research-analysis/opa-surveys/status-of-forces-surveys

U.S. Department of Defense, Office of People Analytics, "Workplace and Gender Relations Survey of Military Members," webpage, undated-c. As of April 5, 2024: https://www.opa.mil/research-analysis/opa-surveys/workplace-and-gender-relations-survey-of-military-members

U.S. Department of Defense, Office of People Analytics, *Defense Organizational Climate Survey (DEOCS) Redesign: Phase 1 Overview Report*, October 2021.

U.S. Department of Defense, Office of People Analytics, *2022 Service Academy Gender Relations Survey*, March 2023.

U.S. Government Accountability Office, *Domestic Abuse: Actions Needed to Enhance DOD's Prevention, Response, and Oversight*, U.S. Government Printing Office, GAO-21-289, May 2021.

U.S. Government Accountability Office, *Sexual Harassment and Assault: The Army Should Take Steps to Enhance Program Oversight, Evaluate Effectiveness, and Identify Reporting Barriers*, U.S. Government Printing Office, GAO-22-104673, May 2022.

Wolters, Heather, Patricia Kannapel, Peggy Golfin, Adam Clemens, Shannon Desrosiers, Thomas Geraghty, Christopher Gonzales, and Kim Fletcher, *Identifying Cross-Cutting Risk and Protective Factors and Prevention Principles for Multiple Harmful Behaviors*, Center for Naval Analyses, January 2023.

Womack Army Medical Center, "e-Profile," webpage, undated. As of June 25, 2024: https://womack.tricare.mil/Health-Services/Readiness/e-Profile